THE BUSINESS OF INVENTION

For Chlöe and Linzi

THE BUSINESS OF INVENTION

How to turn a patentable idea into a profitable product

Patrick Lawrence

2000

First published in Great Britain in 1997 by Management Books 2000 Ltd,
Cowcombe House,
Cowcombe Hill,
Chalford,
Gloucestershire GL6 8HP
Tel: 01285-760722. Fax: 01285-760708
e-mail: mb2000@compuserve.com

Printed and bound in Great Britain by Astron On-Line, Letchworth

British Library Cataloguing in Publication Data is available

ISBN 1-85252-203-8

Contents

PART ONE

The Business of
Invention

Introduction

There has never been a better time to be a British inventor. In the United Kingdom there are now a large number of organisations dedicated to helping independent inventors. In 1991, the Innovation Unit was set up by the DTI to encourage a positive attitude towards industrial innovation within manufacturing industry throughout Great Britain. The compelling need for new ideas was officially recognised. In consequence banks are now increasingly open to credible proposals from inventors and in some cases have formalised the channels through which these applications can be made. Innovation Centres and Enterprise Agencies have been set up regionally, and a number of national competitions offer the inventor an opportunity to present his ideas. The climate has become conducive to creativity for those with inventive imaginations.

But being an inventor is immensely difficult, or more precisely the act of making money out of an invention is difficult. No business enterprise demands such a broad spectrum of practical abilities. To turn an original idea into a commercial product capable of producing a return on its investment requires enormous resources, both tangible and intangible. Of all the private patents filed by individuals at the Patent Office, perhaps only ten per cent will proceed to grant and maybe only five per cent of those will go on to make any real money for their owners (half a per cent!). This figure partly illustrates the non-commercial prospect of the average invention; but to a greater extent it shows that most inventors are just not up to the task. Very few people are both richly creative in their imaginations and sufficiently entrepreneurial in their abilities to achieve a result.

The purpose of this book is to focus on the objective of making money from inventions, and to suggest a number of possible sources of help and financial support for the inventor. Of course, inventors come in all guises, from the legendary wizard in the garden shed, to the scientist-engineer in the research lab. But wherever they come from, it is a truism that most inventions lose money. Making a proving model, paying for and servicing a patent, improving and progressing an idea towards commercial viability, all cost inventors serious money and all too often there is zero return. Eventually their idea dies a premature death and they give up in disgust, disillusioned by their endeavours. This is the common experience. Statistically, people would be better off trying to make a living out of doing the lottery or betting their savings on the horses. There are gamblers who do just that, of course, but they are very astute and leave little to chance. They pursue their goal with a single-minded determination. Inventors who want to make money out of their inventions had better do likewise because, to the same degree, the odds are against them.

However, help is at hand. The heart of this book is the section entitled 'Help for the Inventor'. The most important single thing that inventors must understand is that they cannot go it alone; this will almost certainly lead to failure. Provided they can get a patent granted on their invention, by which time it should have demonstrated some commercial potential, they will have a valuable property which they can then exchange for investment and assistance. The judicious exchange of personal equity in an invention in favour of money and expertise is perhaps the finest line the lone inventor can draw. Provided the value of his remaining equity exceeds the equivalent of his original equity every time he trades it in, he has made a worthwhile deal. In other words, one hundred per cent of a company worth ten thousand pounds is less valuable than fifty per cent of a company worth eighty thousand, or twenty per cent of a company worth half a million pounds.

Hanging on to equity at all costs is futile and counterproductive. Invariably it leads to failure. Of course, it is often difficult to quantify the true value added to your invention when you give up equity, particularly if it is in exchange for a service such as product development by a design consultant; but inventors must assess what the service is worth to them and set their sights accordingly. Besides, the other great advantage to the inventor, in addition to the added value of the investment, is the actual vested interest of the investor. The more people there are who have a practical commitment to the product, the better its chances of success.

But the very act of inventing – creating a new product or concept from the imagination – is intoxicating. That first rush of excitement that follows the germination of an idea is something that can propel an inventor into an unknown world full of adventure, opportunity and risk. The danger is that most inventors are convinced they are on to a winner from the outset and that only a matter of time will make them rich. The very reverse is true. The average inventor is not unlike an unguided missile, using up precious energy and resources in a vain attempt to reach an ill-defined target and doomed to burn itself out uselessly in the wilderness: a Cruise missile, with a built-in route map, has a much better chance of finally reaching its goal.

Unfortunately, it is impossible to study the business of invention academically. No one in our society is able to become a fully qualified, professionally-accredited inventor. The trade of the inventor (in some cases it can become a profession, if only by virtue of the fact that some of us do earn our living by it), is relegated to the realms of the lunatic fringe. It may seem strange, considering our much-lauded national faculty for invention, that when even the most arcane of subjects can be studied, such as parapsychology, there is still no University or College course in the UK on inventing. The truth is that no one sets out to be an inventor; they tend to come upon it in early middle age and invariably through some professional or leisure experience. But once the inventive imagination has been awakened, some people find that they can invent at will. Give them a problem and they'll find the solution.

In very rare instances it can lead to a new and lucrative way of life but, for the majority, it is a dangerous discovery. A small clearing in the commercial jungle suddenly emerges. It looks enticing... Surely it would do no harm to step off the beaten track for a moment and explore it? But the path leads ever onwards and upwards and soon other paths begin to appear.... For a handful of inventors, what starts as an adventure can develop into a prosperous and fulfilling enterprise; for others, it leads only into a vale of tears. This book is designed to provide some insight into that adventure, and point out the perils and pitfalls lurking along the way. However, with intuition, initiative, enterprise and imagination, coupled with a fierce determination, you may be among the lucky few who eventually find the end of their own golden rainbow.

Happy – and successful – inventing!

1

On Being an Inventor

Being an inventor is a glamorous business, or so we are led to believe. The successful inventor is invariably hailed as a genius; but the notion has become something of a cliché which is rarely borne out by the facts. Nevertheless, the prospect of becoming rich and famous through invention remains a persuasive fantasy. People see themselves as being in humdrum jobs even though they are highly qualified and well paid. The prospect of inspirational creativity producing bountiful rewards is a compelling aspiration. Kept initially at arm's length and looked upon benignly as something of a crank, an inventor who becomes successful is suddenly transformed into a mastermind and held up as an example to all. Hitting upon a winning idea and turning it into riches is like finding the key to Aladdin's cave: countless daydreams are fired by these all-too rare stories of success.

But inventing is a serious business that has been central to the ascent of man. The artificial, material world consists entirely of inventions, from the wheel to the magnetic resonance imager. Finding ways of converting natural materials into practical products, useful to mankind, has been fundamental to civilisation since the dawn of history. The more developed societies now inhabit a man-made material world of almost incomprehensible complexity and yet for the most part it is merely taken for granted. The microchip, for instance, has changed the way we live and work in a single generation; yet human beings have embraced this electronic miracle almost as a matter of course, without a moment's misgivings. It has ever been so.

Pause for a moment and consider the Victorian era, let us say in the early 1890s, just about a hundred years ago... The following products either did not exist, or were still in their infancy: the aeroplane, motor car, telephone, radio, television, film, video, cassette player, computer, calculator, photocopier, word processor, laser, washing machine, microwave, fridge and even the material that makes them all possible: plastics. Then there are the medical advances – anaesthetics, antibiotics, vaccines, insulin... The list is endless. All these products are now so 'essential' to our modern world that life would be practically intolerable for most of us without them; a person born in the 1890s – and there are increasing numbers of centenarians surviving – would have known a time when none of these incredible advances existed.

All these amazing creations can invariably trace their origins to the mind of a singular individual – an inventor. Nowadays, inventors tend to regard the golden age of invention as over. In a sense they are right. The days when ideas such as the jet engine, the hovercraft or the photocopier could be conceived and developed into commercial products through the intervention of one man are past. Nowadays, only global corporations have the capacity to develop such marvels as the body scanner or the compact disc. More's the pity, for it is recognised that corporations lack completely the inspirational creativity of the maverick. They do not possess the natural capacity for pure invention.

The individual imagination, however, remains alive and well. The impulse to discover something new is a powerful motivator. All that the modern inventor needs to consider is what, for him, is logistically and economically feasible. In a sense, he must lower his sights. But once he has a clear perception of what is possible, the opportunities are boundless.

Where to begin?

There are two areas of invention that remain fertile ground for the individual: the consumer invention and the industrial invention. This book concerns itself primarily with the former. Industrial inventions tend to come from the research departments of academic institutions. Scientific research is directed at specific targets with the assumption that the invention, when it comes, will find a ready market. Going on to develop a business around such an invention is examined very effectively in John Allen's excellent book, *Starting a Technology Business*. With consumer inventions the situation is reversed. Inventing is the easy part, but putting your idea into production and marketing it is beset with difficulty.

Consumer inventions come in a complex range of shapes and sizes, from the fairly sophisticated Baby Buggy, through the somewhat simpler Workmate, to a rudimentary single moulding like the Frisbee. This is the natural domain of the lone inventor. However, inventions involving basic mechanics or electronics are just as feasible, so long as the end-product remains uncomplicated. Other areas open to the inventive imagination are ideas that can adapt and enhance established industrial processes. Extruded plastic netting was invented by one man, zip-up plastic bags by another. These types of products can be developed quite effectively by an individual. The inventive step is seeing how existing principles can be modified to produce an original product. It is one of the areas in which the inventor has every chance of coming up with an idea that is independently manageable.

But no matter how much the world may be filled with original products, what is clear is that inventors will continue to come up with some startling discoveries. Often these inventions are so simple that the average person is surprised not to have thought of it themselves. In retrospect, it seems so obvious. The extending dog-lead and the weekend cat-feeder are two good examples of products that became immediate commercial successes as soon as they appeared in the shops. Behind these and similar success stories there is often a tale of trial and error, and tenacity in the face of daunting obstacles that the inventor has had to overcome to bring his brainchild to market.

Notwithstanding the quality of the invention, the inventor must pursue his objective with a single-minded determination if he is to succeed where others so often have failed before him. Herein, however, lies a danger; although tenacity and determination are essential for success, blind faith is a prescription for disaster. Before long, the inventor must seek out informed opinion as to the validity of his invention.

What went wrong?

Inventions fail for a number of reasons – clearly, commercial inadequacy is one of them. Technical solutions to hypothetical problems are merely of academic interest, however intriguing in themselves. An invention must satisfy an authentic need if it is to succeed in the marketplace. Often, a single factor is sufficient to extinguish what is otherwise a wonderful idea; simple competition is the most common. If an invention is an improvement on an existing product, it must be irresistibly different. Established products hold entrenched positions in their markets and can normally see off a new rival with ease. Consumers must be enticed to switch to something new. To amuse, astonish, enchant or intrigue can sometimes be sufficient; but plain, practical usefulness holds a powerful appeal. Merely satisfying an old need in a new way is not enough, particularly without an improvement in price, but a dramatic and elegant improvement in performance can work miracles in the marketplace. A remarkable example of this is the Screwpull bottle opener, a method of drawing a cork out of a bottle of wine without actually having to pull it out by hand. By continuing to wind the handle, the cork climbs up the screw and out of the bottle without effort or damage to itself in anyway. The invention has become indispensable to wine enthusiasts the world over. Another clever product is the Magican tin opener, which takes the lid off a tin can in such an elegant fashion that at first it appears improbable. Both these products require minimal effort in their execution; each has become a huge commercial success – in spite of the fact that perfectly adequate methods of opening tin cans and bottles of wine have existed for ages.

There is a raft of other reasons why inventions fail. It is stating the obvious that an invention must actually work if it is to succeed. Sometimes an invention never manages to overcome some key technical obstacle in its development and has to be abandoned. And from time to time a product appears that works perfectly well under normal conditions, but fails at the limit. In certain situations this can be dangerous, and should there be a accident the product is finished forever. A good example of this was the beautiful, bug-eyed Optica Low-Altitude Spotter Plane – a revolutionary aircraft and a wonderful invention in so many ways. One of its principal features was a very low stall speed. However, when first tested by the Dorset Police it fell out of the sky and killed the crew. It never recovered from this catastrophe, even though it was suspected that the pilot, rather than the aircraft, was to blame.

The Optica is an extreme example; but if a product fails to live up to its claim it will quickly be spurned by the consumer. One of the greatest success stories of recent years is the Post-It Note, that little yellow adhesive notepad that appears in every office throughout the world. Nothing could be simpler, but the secret of its success is that it never fails, regardless of the conditions. If the adhesive gave out from time to time and the note fell to the floor, the irritation factor would erode the credibility of the product to the point where eventually it would disappear, regardless of its obvious usefulness. Instead, you cannot escape them anywhere. The importance of reliability, leading to indispensability, cannot be overemphasised.

A product can also fail on aesthetic grounds. When LCD watches first appeared in the early 1980s, they were all the rage. But somehow they did not have quite the visual charm of the old analogue type. Then when quartz crystal technology came along to assure its accuracy, the traditional style of watch, often with Roman numerals, quickly reasserted itself to the almost complete elimination of its upstart digital rival. Good aesthetics can maximise sales and there are plenty of products about that are sold almost exclusively on their design appeal. In fact, sometimes they are not very useful in themselves but they stimulate a desire to possess, and people buy them as a result. The little Plus Office Kit from Japan was a good example;

and how many people are persuaded to buy a new pocket calculator from time to time, even when they possess half a dozen others already?

Another reason products can fail is through changes in consumer perceptions. Environmental issues now play an important part in public awareness. The detachable, ring-pull can-opener has been outlawed in some States in America, and beware any product that uses expanded polystyrene in its manufacture. An international outcry has followed the invention, in California, of the self-cooling drinks can: its coolant HFC gas is said to be three and a half thousand times more potent a global warming agent than CO_2. Inventions that tend to create litter, too, are increasingly unacceptable.

Finally, there are products that fail even though millions of pounds have been bet on them. A certain Dr Nims, from Hong Kong, came up with a camera with two lenses that gave a 3D effect to the photographic print. The technology was seductive. A public company was floated to raise development capital and at one point it reached a value of a hundred million pounds on the stock market, even though not a single camera had yet been sold. When the Nimslo was finally launched, the public took one look, shook their heads and walked away. The Nimslo camera was a complete commercial failure, although investors had predicted a bonanza of Polaroid proportions.

The technology behind the miniature flat-screen television so enthralled electrical engineers worldwide that they could not resist developing it, despite indications that the market was strictly limited. Since being launched it has achieved only minuscule sales and is still regarded as something of a gimmick. Sir Clive Sinclair's C5 Electric Pedal Car was also a commercial disaster. And recently he has had to abandon another of his environmentally friendly creations, the Zike Rechargeable Pedal Bike – brilliant design and technology notwithstanding. The fact is, no one can predict what is going to work in the marketplace and premonitions of failure are all too often fulfilled.

Flawed inventions though are only half the problem: inventors themselves complete the picture. Almost every inventor starts out with the staple daydream. Once he has got his invention right, some eager manufacturer will take it up, offer him a lucrative licence agreement, and send him on his way with a sinecure of royalties for a lifetime of leisure. It is a cruel myth and one that needs to be exposed. The following chapter, 'The Reluctant Manufacturer', sets out to dispel the delusion in some detail.

An objective view

There remains a dichotomy in inventing which is hard to reconcile. On the one hand, the inventor must be passionate about his invention, enthusiastic and full of conviction, dedicated to its success; yet, on the other, he must be coldly analytical, able to distance himself from it completely and examine it with critical dispassion.

There is only one way to do this and that is to put the two states into separate compartments and make sure that the latter precedes the former. As much time as possible should be allowed to pass between the original concept and its further development. Most inventors are not short of ideas and are able to think them through reasonably well before investing too much time on them. There should be nothing more than a bit of development work just to prove the principle. Once the inventor is satisfied that his idea is sound, his best approach is to lay it down in the cellar of his mind for as long as possible and give it time to mature. Hand it over to the subconscious to work on for a while – a year being about right.

When eventually you re-examine it, you will be astonished at how different it appears and how removed at first you feel from it. At that very moment you will know the true value of your idea. If the earlier excitement that you first felt at its conception comes surging back, then maybe you do have something worth pursuing. But is more likely you will wonder why you ever seriously considered the idea in the first place; it now seems rather superficial and of dubious commerciality. Of course, this process may be impractical for one reason or another, but keeping a rolling portfolio of ideas which are given due time to ripen is one way of clearly identifying the potential winners.

Every inventor has his 'hundred per cent' invention – the one that, above all others, is going to make him rich. Certainly, his remaining

19

ideas have relative merit and he can rate them down the scale accordingly: eighty per cent, fifty per cent, twenty per cent. But his judgement is based only on his own experiences and perceptions of reality. By another, his hundred per cent invention might be rated at only seventy per cent – although that same inventor smugly clings to his own hundred per cent idea. But then he is also unaware that a professional inventor, with years of experience behind him would give him only a fifty percent chance of success. In fact, even the professional who makes a living out of inventing can delude himself into believing his brainchild is going to be a surefire success, when in fact it fails dismally in the marketplace. Years of experience notwithstanding, nothing is more uncertain than the business of invention.

So,how does an inventor judge the real merit of his invention? In a word, through the affirmation of others. Part Two of this book, 'Help for the Inventor', provides a carefully selected list of organisations and individuals who have some remit to advise inventors. It is essential they turn to this source for assistance. Sometimes the advice may not be to their liking; it is galling to have spent time and money developing an idea, only to be told by a complete stranger that it is worthless. A second and third opinion should be sought and perhaps a more sympathetic appraisal may be forthcoming, but all inventors are strongly urged to take heed of constructive criticism. It may save them a lot of heartache, not to mention money, in the long run.

The inescapable reality of professional inventing is that it does cost serious money. To begin with, your engagement is low; especially if you have made the model yourself and have not yet applied for a patent. Your vested interest in the invention remains modest and is unlikely to cloud your thinking. But as it develops and your involvement increases, so the idea becomes ever-harder to forsake. Commitment to your product grows in direct proportion to your investment. It is a dangerous spiral which even the most level-headed can become affected by. There lies a thin line between probable failure and possible success. It is crucial to come to an early decision. A probable failure must be ruthlessly rooted out, a possible success judiciously cultivated. Half-measures are pointless. Any money spent on a bad idea is wholly irredeemable and on a good idea the investment may become enormous before any return is realised. The business of invention has a pitiless appetite for money.

Seeking support for your invention

So how should an inventor decide whether or not to go ahead? Apart from seeking outside advice and doing a patent search to establish the novelty of his idea, he must look to himself for the final answer. Once he is convinced that his idea can go the distance, he must ask himself whether he has got what it takes to get there also. No invention, however brilliant, ever sold itself. The world will not beat a path to your door, you can depend on that. Offering your prototype to potential licensees is doomed to failure. Even with the assistance of a professional broker, an unproven invention stands little chance of being taken up. In a later chapter, 'Growing your Own Invention', a somewhat idealised scenario is described for achieving a result. It is not wide of the mark.

Different inventions will require their own variations, but in every case a partner should be sought. The inventor must decide for himself whom to enlist in his search for success. He has a number of sources to choose from, but anything less than complete commitment on his part and those of his associates is pointless. There are only two sound reasons for developing an invention: either to make money, or as an engaging, intellectual hobby. Being a hobby inventor can be a pleasurable pastime. Proving to yourself that an idea can be made to work is very gratifying. Using it yourself and making a few models for your friends is rewarding. Getting publicity in your local paper, going in for invention competitions, even exhibiting at the famous inventors' fairs in Europe, such as Concours Lepine in Paris or the International Exhibition of Inventions in Geneva, will not cost you too much money. Drafting your own patent application and filing it at the Patent Office requires next to nothing in terms of investment, provided you do not use the services of a patent agent. But do not delude yourself: at this level you have little chance of commercial success and you must keep your expenses in check. Like all hobbies, it is a diversion to be kept in proportion to the pleasures derived, and enjoyed safe in the knowledge that ninety five per cent of all inventions have no prospects anyway in the marketplace, regardless of the degree of effort put into in them.

But, for the serious inventor, the time has now come to move on, despite the risks that lie ahead. Provided he is determined to go the distance, it is hoped that this book can furnish him with an effective route map through the jungle. All along there are difficulties and dangers and it is important that he keeps his eye on the prize and his attention focused on the main objective. It is an exciting adventure, but with no guarantees of success he had better start seeking out all those best suited to bringing his brainchild into reality.

2

The Reluctant Manufacturer

Every inventor has his dream. They come in a variety of forms, but invariably involve a rich lifestyle supported by a copious flow of royalties from a benefactor that will enable them to indulge their every desire. The source of this munificence is a manufacturer.

Reality in fact is very different; manufacturers rarely buy inventions, at least not from inventors. The manufacturer is a much maligned and reluctant player in the whole business of invention. He will, it is true, generally acknowledge and on occasion seriously consider the unsolicited submissions of outside individuals, but he is rarely disposed to actually purchase them. After all, he has not invited inventors to send him their proposals, nor has he a need to. He would not employ people in his own costly research and development department if he felt he would better served obtaining his new product ideas from elsewhere.

Most manufacturers feel more comfortable with their own R & D facility where they can be certain that the focus will be directed into areas more suited to their commercial requirements. The outside inventor is a wild card – the joker in the pack. He might just have a part to play, and on occasion a valuable one at that; one that could even rekindle the fortunes of a company. But the manufacturer might as well search for a nugget of gold by the light of the moon as investigate methodically every independent idea that is offered to him. The chances are so remote that he will find a winner that he can be forgiven for viewing the activities of outside inventors with some scepticism. The average inventor, on the other hand, sees things rather differently. How could an enlightened manufacturer not marvel at his creation; surely he cannot be so short-sighted? Anyway, if one turns him down, then another will take him up. Sooner or later a licensee must be found; it is just a matter of time and persistence. Thus the innocent inventor sets out fired with enthusiasm. He compiles a list of all the manufacturers he can think of who make products comparable to his own invention. He sends out a series of letters outlining his idea in some detail and describes what it is designed to do. But he will be dismayed by the response. Half the manufacturers will not reply at all, and those that do will send him what is clearly a standard letter inviting him to sign a confidential non-disclosure document and advising him to apply for a patent before they will look at his idea. The inventor has had his first taste of the interminable delays and disappointments that lie in store for him.

It's good, but it's not one of ours...

Most industrialists will admit that they would rather not deal with inventors at all; they are frankly too much of a liability and take up valuable time. In today's high-tech, fast-moving companies such as the automotive, electronic or computer industries, the research departments of international organisations are light-years ahead of the pedestrian inventor. It is so improbable that the man in the street will think of something that they have completely overlooked, that every creative idea is viewed with deep suspicion. Most external submissions are examined at least superficially by the appropriate experts within the company. But if these specialists raise any objections whatever, be they production problems, technical questions or commercial complications, the idea will go no further. An invention submitted from outside finds no natural allies within a company and is viewed with, at best, indifference, and at worst, derision. This is where the notorious NIH syndrome manifests itself.

The notion of NIH (Not Invented Here) has been around for a long time. Inventors through the ages have complained bitterly of the indifference of their quarry, the ideal manufacturer, and his lofty dismissal of their ideas. They have found it hard to understand why manufacturers adopt such a high-handed attitude towards them and are so ill-disposed to their wonderful creations. But the manufacturer has his own agenda, and it would be prudent for the ambitious inventor to try to gain some insight into the way companies work.

Manufacturing is no longer what it used to be; technology has changed the whole picture. The globalisation of markets and fierce competition from Japan, Korea and other Far East countries means that the industrial scene is increasingly dominated by giant conglomerates. These major groups operate huge R & D programmes using every means at their disposal to stay one step ahead of their competitors. The motor industry, for instance, works some seven to ten years ahead on its future range of models. It utilises an enormous range of state-of-the-art technology, both in its construction techniques and manufacturing systems. Nothing now escapes the notice of an industry that cannot afford to miss a beat. Every new advance is swept up into the net and picked over for possibilities.

Where have I seen that before?

On the face of it, this competitive world would appear ideal ground for the inventor; after all his stock-in-trade is new ideas. But in reality he is not even in the race. In fact, when it comes to dealing with the big high-tech companies, the innocent inventor is often unaware of the sheer weight of R & D that is going on behind the scenes. The chances of him coming up with something original that is entirely outside the realms of anything the company has thought of before are extremely unlikely. Indeed, one of the principal complaints levelled at inventors by manufacturers is that, for the most part, they are ill-informed. This is no more than stating a fact rather than voicing a criticism – it could hardly be otherwise. A common mistake inventors make is to assume that their idea must be new because it is not on the market. The very reverse is often the case. It is not on the market because it is not new. It is an old idea that has been around for a long time, that has been tried and tested and perhaps even put into production at one point but has been withdrawn because of cost, technical shortcomings or poor performance in the marketplace. An early search at the Patent Office might very well have revealed the prior art.

The fact remains that any new invention submitted by an outsider to a company will be burdened with disadvantages from the outset, regardless of its intrinsic merits. Before being taken on board for examination it will have to run a gauntlet of unbridled criticism. It will find few friends and encounter detractors at every turn. It has the potential to ruffle feathers and bruise egos. Even with a product champion nursing it through the company's corridors of power, it will undergo constant disparagement. As a newcomer, it is on notice of probation until it has proved itself beyond all reasonable doubt. If it does survive this baptism of fire, it will be truly worthy of serious scrutiny. Some good examples can be found in *Breakthroughs!*, by P.R. Nayak and J.M. Ketteringham (Management Books 2000)

The product champion is an essential ally for any new invention. Unfortunately, in almost every case the inventor only has one chance to find and cultivate one such within his chosen company – and that's during his first presentation. Naturally, the more senior his new confederate, the better chance his invention has of surviving its rite of passage. The inventor must sell the idea of his invention to someone who has the authority and conviction to carry it forward. Such a person must then be carefully nurtured by the inventor and kept informed of every development. His role is to act as the foster parent to the product within the company during its infancy.

The problem is in finding the right candidate. Not only must this paragon be someone who believes in the invention completely, and has the power to support it, but he must intimately understand it as well. He will be required continually to fight its corner and, without a detailed knowledge of the invention, he may find himself unable to answer all the probing queries put to him by his less than enthusiastic colleagues. He could even find his professional judgement questioned and his status in the company jeopardised. If he has not got complete conviction and a detailed comprehension of the invention, he might just abandon it to save his face with his peers.

However, a good product champion who stays the course is an invaluable asset for an inventor. He certainly deserves to be treated as such, even to the point of being offered a share of the rewards that may materialise as a result of his efforts. After all, the product champion is the only means the inventor has of maintaining some inside control over the passage of his invention towards corporate acceptance and ultimate commercial development. But an authentic product champion is a very rare creature indeed and any inventor would be well advised to consider carefully whom best to approach from the outset within his chosen company.

The waiting game

Although it is tempting to present your idea to the biggest manufacturer first, this is almost always a mistake. Despite receiving huge numbers of submissions from individuals, and even having a formalised system for dealing with them, they rarely, if ever, buy in ideas from outside. As discussed earlier, their corporate culture effectively prohibits it. In fact, the only realistic chance an inventor has is with a smaller company that has specialist knowledge and up-to-date manufacturing facilities for his product. In a company such as this, often still run by the founder or his successors, your ideal product champion is not only clearly visible, but generally accessible: the managing director.

Once your invention is in the hands of a manufacturer, however, you will be compelled to work to their timetable. The worst part is the waiting; you can depend on it that weeks will pass, sometimes months, before you get any response. You can always politely telephone to remind them of your existence, but in effect there is not a lot more that you can do. Horror stories abound: occasionally, your ideas will have set alarm bells ringing. Corporate patent lawyers can tie up your invention for years, ensuring it never sees the light of day. You can become enmired in country-by-country patent protection cases, until you run out of money or patience and abandon your idea altogether – whereupon it mysteriously appears in the marketplace. You should approach large companies with the utmost caution.

Whenever you contact the company, try always to speak to the same person, indeed it is important that you do. The last thing you want is to start giving an historical account of your invention and its progress through the company to someone entirely unacquainted with it. Even if your product champion would not appear ideal, try to build a personal relationship with him. The more he identifies with you and your invention, the more he is persuaded to work on your behalf. The situation can be very delicate and it is easy to overstep the mark and become a nuisance. Be aware of this and show restraint, but at the same time being overly compliant with the manufacturer's inertia and interminable timetable can work against you. If your idea stays on the shelf for too long it becomes history, both metaphorically and in fact, as it sits there, gathering dust and gradually losing its appeal. You must judge for yourself what is right and reasonable and keep the manufacturer aware of your own needs.

If you are one of the very lucky few who gets a manufacturer to go into production with your invention, all your patience and persistence will have paid off. But if you fail, you can console yourself in the certain knowledge that you are one among many whose ideas have been rejected. Basically there are seven distinct reasons why manufacturers rarely buy inventions from individuals:

- The idea turns out not to be new .
- The idea is technically unworkable
- The development costs are too high
- The manufacturing costs are too high
- Market research proves unpromising
- The invention eclipses the manufacturer's existing product
- 'NIH' – the invention fails to survive its rite of passage through the company.

Be sure of your ground

There is one more problem relating to companies in the modern age that increases even further the chances for irrational rejection: industry is dynamic. In the old days, companies were built on bedrock and run by the successors of the founding fathers. They were securely fixed in the firmament of the industrial order of the day and on the whole grew organically. But in the late 20th century all that has been swept away and the situation is far more fluid. Turn your back, and the company has merged, been sold off, or taken over. Famous names, now owned by multinationals, are merely component parts of huge conglomerates. Where once they were independent planets revolving in fixed orbits, now they are mere satellites in a far bigger galaxy. Your product champion, too – how safe is his job, in an era of 'downsizing' and 'flat management structures'?

We live in the age of the takeover, the merger and the management buy-out, when an inventor's carefully cultivated contact can quite unexpectedly lose his job or be moved elsewhere, leaving no one to manage his projects. Even if he remains in place, he can find himself suddenly answerable to a higher authority. His lines of communication can be stretched beyond his control and perhaps become located in another office or worse still, another country. Just when things were beginning to look promising and on the threshold of a breakthrough, a change of direction, a new corporate order, a dictate from on high, can pull the rug from under him and the inventor is back where he began, with a marooned and valueless invention.

Despite this discouraging picture of the improbabilities of successfully marketing your invention through a manufacturer, it is not impossible to achieve a result. After all, as we shall see later on, it is the job of invention brokers to try to make a living out of it. If your chosen manufacturer appears half interested in your idea, find out what his reservations are about it as well. If he feels the product has potential but is unsure of the market, offer to supply him with further information. If he thinks it is going to be too expensive to manufacture, offer to redesign it to make it simpler or cheaper. If he is worried about where the development capital is going to come from, remind him that he can sometimes get a development grant through his regional Business Link. In other words, do his thinking for him. Demonstrate that your inventiveness and enterprise do not stop at the idea itself. Become part of the team, get on the inside, become indispensable, become your own product champion within the company. This is not an easy thing to do, but if you can it is an excellent way to keep your invention alive within the company until you are able to steer it into a licence agreement and finally into full-scale commercial production.

Although it is true that the chances of success are slim, there is no doubt that, for almost every inventor, the idea of a licence agreement for his invention with a suitable manufacturer remains the ideal. Indeed, the most successful professional inventors derive most of their income from royalties. How then can they achieve this when it seems that the route ahead is barred? Well, they have acquired a fundamental insight. A product that has proved its potential in the marketplace, through genuine sales to the public, is suddenly an attractive proposition for a manufacturer. If you really want the businessl world to come knocking on your door, you had better have something commercially credible to offer it.

3

The Elementary Invention

Inventing is easy if you have the gift: inventors are born and not made. Like all disciplines, invention needs to be practised to achieve results; but the imagination is a powerful tool when focused clearly. Mere reveries about fanciful products of no functional use are the stuff of daydreams. The serious inventor who means to make money out of his idea must subjugate his visions to a critical sense of practical reality.

The inventive mind has certain abilities, the most important being the capacity to visualise. Identifying a problem and devising a solution that seeks to solve it is a facility not given to everybody, but without it one cannot invent. Many inventors will tell you that they are able to picture an imaginary object in their minds as plainly as if it were on a display screen in front of them. It is viewed in three dimensions; the details are quite distinct. Once the image is in full focus, it is ready to be put to the test. Plug it in and see if it works – well up to a point, but not well enough. Modify this; simplify that; play with the model until it performs. Eureka! you've got it. Nothing surpasses the pleasure of these creative visual mind games.

Gifted inventors are hugely prolific; their ability to resolve functional problems in their heads is so well developed that new ideas spill over each other. Finding solutions to practical problems is not the

31

challenge: the difficulty is in deciding which one to develop. But here the professional has an advantage; for, as everyone knows who has tried to market his invention, taking it to the starting gate is a far remove from riding it past the winning post. Your professional inventor has no illusions. He may possess a rich portfolio of ideas, but picking the right one is the problem; after all, any one might have the potential to make him a fortune. But which? It is a crucial judgement for it is going to require his total commitment for many years to come. And even then, it's all a wild venture.

This chapter is designed to offer some insights into the sort of inventions that can create real wealth. It is important to understand that there are no half-measures. Either a pastime or a profession, inventing offers no middle ground. Being a hobby inventor is fine, so long as you don't get drawn into the black hole of patenting without the necessary means to develop and market your invention, or investing serious money on a doomed idea.

Who needs another mousetrap?

Invent for need: it might seem obvious, but it is amazing how many inventors ignore the rule. But the notion of need is subjective until it is confirmed by market research. The job of the researcher is to find out for a manufacturer if his product is likely to sell. What the manufacturer wants is a market niche. The smallest viable size of that niche is determined by the value of the product. Any manufacturer would be unwise to commit himself to production until he is confident of the market. On a much smaller scale the inventor must do the same. Quantifying the commercial need for a new idea is just the beginning. If the size of the market that your invention is designed to satisfy is not established from the outset, then you may be heading for disaster. Nothing is more unforgiving than the marketplace, and if the need has been misinterpreted, overestimated or merely overlooked, the cost of your oversight will soon become painfully apparent.

But what is meant by need in this context? Need is objective and need is subjective, and the two are inextricably mixed together. For need is also desire motivated by personal taste, and the actual aesthetics of a product can create a powerful urge in someone to possess it regardless of its actual usefulness. Imagine you need to buy a new kettle: you start by deciding what sort you want, a hob kettle or an electric kettle. This is the easy part: an electric kettle is so much more convenient. The next choice is simple enough also: a jug kettle is more modern and stylish than the traditional type. You set off with confidence to your local superstore where you are confronted with more than twenty different styles of jug kettle appearing altogether much the same. Then, over in the corner, something brightly coloured catches your eye: it is an anodised aluminium hob kettle, mixed in primary colours, with a plastic steam whistle attached to the spout. You pick it up and examine it carefully. It is very beautiful, but much too expensive. You put it down and return to the rows of ubiquitous jug kettles lined up like sentries in uniform. Twenty minutes later you walk out of the store with the aluminium kettle in a box under your arm. Aesthetics have won the day against all practical considerations.

So need is necessary, but in itself is not enough. Desire is built in through design, and any manufacturer of consumer products who does not appreciate the importance of these two factors in consumer choice had better put up his shutters before the receiver does.

A question of chemistry

Identifying need is one thing, carefully creating desirability is quite another, and by combining the two into a successful product a sort of alchemy is achieved. But the inventor who wants to come up with a real money spinner must go a stage further: for the inventions that really make millions are those which anticipate and satisfy a need that has never before been fully recognised. Indeed, creating a need where none was apparent is the traditional domain of the individual inventor. Think of the Workmate, think of the Baby Buggy, think of the Flymo, think of plastic netting, think of Bubble Wrap; all these products were so radically new at their inception that they created vastly more need than their outdated predecessors had been required to satisfy. In other words,

Bubble Wrap now wraps products that formerly were not wrapped at all and the Flymo mows areas of grass previously inaccessible to a motor mower. No manufacturer ever imagined these wonderful products before he saw them being demonstrated by their inspired creators.

Another important characteristic an invention must have is to be commercial in itself. An invention that could go on to become a successful product but is difficult to sell as a concept may never be given the chance. For example, a qualified electrical engineer came up with a brilliantly simple idea, a method of printing a conductor between the end caps of a standard 13-amp electrical fuse. This conductor was applied in metallic ink on the outside of the fuse, connecting the metal end caps and then printed over with white ink. When the main fuse failed the current immediately travelled up the false fuse and burnt it out, leaving a line of scorched ink that was now clearly visible. How many people would wish to buy such a product? At a negligible increase in cost it could save the whole tiresome business of trying to establish by trial and error whether the fuse in an appliance really has failed or whether there is something wrong with the appliance itself. Despite persistence, the inventor failed to find a manufacturer and the product remains to this day commercially unavailable. Needless to say, the reasons given by all the leading manufacturers for not taking it up were as varied as they were shortsighted. But the plain truth is that, despite an overwhelming desire to put the thing into production yourself and prove them all wrong, with this sort of invention there is no way it can be done by a lone individual unless he becomes a fuse manufacturer himself.

Although the odds against selling an invention of this kind are acute, there is another type which is next-to impossible. This is a bolt-on improvement to a manufacturer's existing product. Keyless electric drill chucks have been developed and patented by countless inventors over the years, but none was ever taken up directly by a manufacturer. Yet nowadays most manufacturers market their own. Likewise, the automotive industry almost never buys mechanical or electrical improvements to their motor vehicles; although car accessories that can be bought separately in high street shops offer a potential source of lucrative ideas for the independent inventor.

Room for improvement

As was indicated earlier, technical inventions, as opposed to those aimed at consumers, are really outside the scope of this book, mainly because marketing them is so very different. In the first place, they rarely consist of a standalone product. Even a revolutionary electrical motor, complete though it might be in itself, is not an independent product. It only serves its purpose when attached to something else. Most technical inventions come out of research establishments where the inventor is employed as a researcher. Very few individuals have the necessary resources to achieve a technical breakthrough on their own, although it is always individuals who initiate them. Often the market for such inventions is clearly defined from the outset, and once a result has been reached and the technology perfected, the intellectual property can be licensed out by such august organisations as the British Technology Group.

Unlike consumer products, the selling of a technological improvement may be the easy part. For it is true that, from time to time, researchers do set up in business to exploit their own ideas – indeed some of them are very good at it, attracting substantial grants from the DTI by winning, for example, one of the awards available under the SMART scheme. But the problems they encounter are not at all the same as those that face the ordinary inventor. What concerns us here are consumer inventions, products that can be produced and packaged and sold retail to the general public. From a practical point of view, it is apparent that the independent inventor should direct his attention towards this broad category of ideas; after all, the scope of opportunity is unlimited.

Once again I wish to emphasise this question of need. Many inventors satisfy themselves that a product does not exist merely because they have never seen it. Nothing could be more illusory. Shops and particularly superstores only stock successful products; they have no room for the rest. Any inventor who has ever got as far as offering his DIY device to the likes of B&Q or Argos will know that he must firmly establish market potential before he will be considered for inclusion in their catalogues and even then he may be rejected on the grounds that his is a one-product company. The smaller independents are more flexible and indeed discover many new products at trade fairs which they can sometimes be persuaded to try out with their customers.

To begin with, the inventor must be aware of what is available. It is difficult to come up with a product that nobody else has thought of before. The world is awash with fashionable products. Apart from Europe and America, Japan and China, the countries of the Pacific Rim are pumping out products at a furious rate. Of course, much of it is copycat stuff if not straightforwardly counterfeit. As soon as a new product becomes successful, everyone is onto it, but at the same time the search is always on for the next new craze. For as anyone knows, the first in the field reaps the richest rewards. When Professor Rubik came up with his famous cube, he patented it only in Hungary. By the time it was discovered by Tom Kramer of Seven Towns, the patent was worthless. Through swift and energetic marketing worldwide, Kramer was able to control perhaps one third of all the cubes sold in the first two years of the craze, which amounted to many millions; despite the fact that scores of Asian manufacturers had begun making and selling them at hugely discounted prices. It is essential for the inventor to be informed. To use a tired old cliché, there's no point in reinventing the wheel.

Apart from a preliminary expedition to his local consumer trading estate, where an afternoon in the sheds will show him what's available, there are only two sources he needs to investigate. For new product searching, start where the buyers start: at the trade fairs. The bigger and more international they are, the better. The NEC in Birmingham stages some excellent exhibitions but they do not compare with the giant industrial and consumer trade fairs in Europe, particularly in Germany. If you want to see a cornucopia of consumer products, go to the International Spring Fair in Frankfurt, but allow at least three days just to absorb it all.

The second place to look is the British Patent Library in London – where a search for prior art at the Patent Office is liable to reveal some unexpected and perhaps unwelcome surprises...

Provided the two exercises taken together uncover nothing too alarming, the inventor must next ask himself seriously why his invention does not already exist? Can it really be that he is the first to have thought of it? Well probably not. But he may just be the first who intends to do something about it. Any inventor who has been in the game for some time will tell you that ideas are "in the ether"... It is a strange phenomenon: no sooner have you thought of something quite new than similar products begin to appear all about you, even though they originate from elsewhere. Indeed, it is the principal reason why an inventor should pursue a new idea with some alacrity. If he is entirely convinced that he is on to a winner, he had better patent it ahead of his peers.

If you haven't invented it, it must exist...

But there may be another good reason why an invention does not already exist: there is no actual need for it. Need is relative, but in commercial terms it is all-important. Inadequate need will result in poor sales and if the product does not turn a profit, it will fail. Manufacturers will estimate the potential market for a new product and then lop off one third. Only if the remaining two thirds still look promising will they be persuaded to put it into production. Otherwise the investment is not worth the risk. However attractive an invention may at first appear, it must make a market to succeed. This is one of the very hardest things for the inventor to accept. He has worked diligently to get his invention perfected; his patent agent assures him he will get a strong patent, the idea works well and is clearly targeted. The principle is seductive, the design is excellent, the price is right. Everyone he shows it to tells him they would buy it – how can it fail? Well, it fails because the market niche is just too small.

This happened some years ago to the inventor of the electric hot-water bottle, a conventional rubber bottle that was sold with the water sealed inside and an electric plug attached to the top. A few minutes plugged into the mains and the water reached boiling point. Unplugged, it turned into a conventional hot water bottle, one that you could even reheat during the night and avoid entirely the hazards of scalding – a sure-fire hit, you might assume. But it failed to reach its sales target and duly perished. Ironically, the gel-filled bottle that you heat up in the microwave oven sells in its hundreds of thousands. Anyone can be forgiven for getting it wrong.

Sir Clive Sinclair is a brilliant man. Some would call him a genius. Certainly he is Britain's highest profile inventor and the only one ever to have received a knighthood for his achievements. At one time his company, Sinclair Electronics, was worth one hundred million pounds on the stock market. He invented the pocket calculator, the first and most widely used of all the consumer inventions based on the microchip. He designed and produced the Sinclair ZX Personal Computer, the first really inexpensive PC to appear in the UK; way back in the 1970s it sold in hundreds of thousands. He seemed all set to become as rich as Croesus. But then he came up with the C5 electric pedal car, which failed dismally in the market place; and, more recently, the Zike Rechargeable Electric Bicycle, for carrying cyclists effortlessly up hills, has fared little better. Even a man of such remarkable talents, with considerable capital at his disposal, can disastrously misjudge the market for a new product – and not just once.

Indeed, so important is it to satisfy a commercial need in order to achieve market success that it is tempting to try to improve only existing products. Inventors are forever looking for a new way of doing an old job. But, as was seen with the Screwpull, unless a new invention of this nature is wholly exceptional, in all probability it will fail. Enticing though it may at first appear, this is not fertile ground for the inventor. What he must do is to discover a niche that is truly new and then fill it with something that is without precedent – what is known as a '*new*' new product. This is the richest vein for the lone inventor, one which he can make his very own virgin territory.

But despite their clear advantages, 'new' new products do have one major drawback: they are difficult to quantify theoretically and even more difficult to establish commercially.

Take your data with a pinch of salt

Market research is unreliable. At one time if you had asked people in the street whether they would buy a little yellow notepad of paper that stuck to things (Post-it Notes) or a device for taking air out of a wine bottle (Vac-U-Van) or a little sliding disc for moving heavy furniture about (Glis-domes), you would probably have received some quizzical looks and sardonic responses. If people cannot clearly visualise a product, their reaction to the idea tends to be instinctively negative. The only way to find out is to try it out – all you have to go on is a hunch. 3M, who were convinced of the potential of Post-it Notes, could not at first persuade people to buy them. Finally they resorted to giving away boxes of samples to every office in their local town with an invitation to come back for more if they wanted them. The only condition was that next time they would have to pay for them. The response was phenomenal. At the other end of the scale, the microwave oven had to overcome powerful consumer resistance in its early days for much the same reason – people could not see the need for it.

Human beings are conservative creatures; they like what they know. But they are inquisitive as well, they need to be persuaded to try out something new and no one persuades them better than their neighbour. An unsolicited testimonial from someone they trust can work wonders, but it takes time to build up a network of neighbours and establishing a new product can be a protracted business. Then, the rewards for success are worth it. Being the first in the field with a new idea that everybody latches on to can give you much more than a running start. Someone once created a fad in America by putting a beach pebble in a box and calling it Pet Rock. Before the next person climbed onto the bandwagon, the game was all-but over, but by then the originator had walked away with a small fortune.

But what does a stone in a box have to do with need? Nothing whatever. We have seen how aesthetics and personal taste play their parts, but so too does novelty. A product that can fascinate, tantalise, charm and amuse the consumer in some way is immensely attractive particularly if is not expensive. A good example of this is the famous Newton's cradle, an exquisitely simple model demonstrating the first law of motion – that every force produces an equal and opposite force. These beautiful but useless devices have sold in their millions for a quarter of a century, not so much as an educational model, but as an executive toy and object of curiosity, livening up the office or domestic scene.

Keep it simple

Thus the inventor can begin to focus his attention. Need, novelty, elegance and absolute originality, and all connected to cost. Perceived value is essential regardless of price; and any product that sells for under £10 has a huge advantage. Most people consider anything costing less than a 'tenner' to be small change, and for a mere 'fiver', all but free – almost an impulse buy. Newsagents are full of novelties in this price range, mostly aimed at parents with small children. Beach shops around the world are packed with products that may well be used only for a single day. The Velcro Scatchball, which in a matter of months appeared in every toy and beach shop around the country, would probably have failed at over £5. And another charming toy that only offers a moment's amusement, but has sold in countless millions, is the little singing top that lights up and plays a simple tune when you spin it. Products like these offer the inventor endless scope to exercise his imagination and pursue his dreams of bountiful fulfilment.

They also offer him something else that is of great importance if he wishes to see his fantasies realised. Whether designing for need or designing for desire, he should keep his inventions as simple as possible. The low-tech, high-volume novelty that can be produced with the minimum of cost and the maximum of expedition – preferably made by a contract manufacturer in China, who can introduce it all over the world in a single season – is the product that could make its inventor a millionaire overnight. And if he can add an element of skill and participation to his invention, he will almost certainly have hit upon a winner. Consider the line up: the Hula Hoop, the Frisbee, Rubik's Cube, Slinkee, Yo-Yo, Scatchball, Roller Blade, Stunt Kite, Skateboard ... the list goes on; and, who knows, you could be the next to add your ingenious invention to this illustrious roll-call of world beating, money-spinning inventions

4

Growing Your Own Invention

The world is full of successful inventions; we meet them every day, at every turn. Walking in an ancient forest of seemingly ageless trees, it seems incredible that all of them started out as tiny seedlings. What is not apparent, as you gaze up into the towering canopy, is how many millions of seedlings have died in the making of that great forest. When it comes to invention, the creation of the 'technosphere', the story is just the same. An inventive notion while sitting in a traffic jam one day can change your life. The 'germination' of the seed of an idea is a perilous moment, the change may not be for the better; but 'great oaks from little acorns grow' – it has ever been so.

Cheer up, it can happen to you...

Nobody thinks of themselves as being an inventor until they become one. It can happen to you quite unexpectedly. Inventing is not seen as a professional activity, any more than is travelling; although it is clear that there are people who do indeed make a living at it. Few activities stray further into the realms of the eccentric than becoming a full-time inventor. The thought of giving up your comfortable job and domestic security after so many years in your chosen profession is beyond serious contemplation.

And yet the thought lingers on... It is a marvellous idea and stands up to scrutiny. The more you think about it the more you like it. And the pleasure of having thought of it in the first place is strangely satisfying. Certainly you have never seen anything like it before. What wonderful advantages it would have over its outmoded predecessors – less expensive, more convenient, environmentally attractive and so simple to manufacture... It is even possible that you are the first person ever to have thought of it! What a seductive reverie.

Over a lunchtime drink in the pub one day you mention it to a close friend. What does he think? Has he ever seen such a thing before? Does he think it would work? His answers are encouraging. Frankly, he thinks it's a wonderful idea and congratulates you on having thought of it in the first place. He tells you you really should do something about it; perhaps patent it and try and get a model made.

The idea begins to engage your mind. The fact is, you are fifty years old and bored with your job. It is well-paid and has given you many years of comfort and security – you have bought a home and raised a family on it – but it has become second nature to you now and has long since ceased to be a challenge. You have reached the top of the tree and there is nowhere else for you to go. You are healthy and in your professional prime. The children are leaving home. What have you got to look forward to now beyond your pension and a comfortable retirement? Surely life must hold out more excitement than just that? Maybe the time has come for a change. And what a change it would be, what a challenge, what a gamble!

But steady on. No point in jumping in too fast when you know nothing about these matters. For one thing, years in your profession have taught you a certain circumspection. Perhaps it is time to talk it over with your wife; you have not mentioned it to her until now. Her reaction surprises you. She has nothing whatever to say about the invention, but plenty to say about your proposal to develop it yourself. It is the first time she has ever imagined you could go off the rails. What's the point of risking all you have both worked for for so long – and for some hairbrained daydream? Pull yourself together and face up to reality.

You need to see a specialist...

It is a sobering moment. Perhaps she is right after all. For a few days your feet stay firmly on the ground. But then you meet your friend again and he asks you how it's going – he really is enthusiastic about it. You ask him to keep quiet about the idea. He promises to do so but urges you strongly to go and see a patent agent. In fact, he has a friend who knows one, he'll give you his number.

A few days later you find yourself in the office of your recommended agent. You have never met a patent agent before. He puts you in mind of a solicitor with a refreshingly positive air about him. You explain your invention but add that you know nothing about patenting. The patent agent appears to think that your idea has promise and would certainly stand a good chance of getting a full patent grant. He outlines the procedures and tells you how much it would cost to have him draw up a specification and file for a patent on your behalf. However, he makes an unexpected proposal. Why not first have a search done for prior art at the Patent Office just to confirm the novelty of your idea? It would cost very little and at least you would find out whether your idea really is original. He will happily undertake it for you. You thank him and go away knowing that you have finally taken your first practical step towards growing your own invention.

However, the idea still remains no more than a concept. You wisely decide to await the result of the patent agent's search. At least that will establish the novelty or otherwise of your invention. A few weeks later your patent agent calls you – he sounds upbeat. He has some good news, he wants to see you. The results of the search look very encouraging. He congratulates you. There is nothing in the dozen or so documents he has before him, describing previously patented ideas in the same general category as yours, that could possible eclipse your invention, except perhaps one, and he is fairly confident he could find a way around it. The position looks promising and he suggests you instruct him to draw up a specification and file an application for a patent right away.

But, as you explain, although the idea is clearly in your head and you have conveyed to him exactly what it is designed to do, it still has no material form. Perhaps you should first make a model of sorts to test out its principles. He agrees and recommends you to a model maker he knows. You visit the model maker. He likes the principle but explains he cannot make a model until he has a detailed drawing of what he is required to make. However, he knows a product designer who might be able to help. You are not at all clear what the designer can do for you, you have vague images of a studio full of people at drawing-boards producing fantastic visions of futuristic products.

You arrive at the studio in good time and are shown into the consulting room where you are asked to wait. You sit down at a large oval polished wooden table with black leather chairs set around it. At one end is aof the room is a large projection screen and at the other an automatic slide projector. In a corner there is a television monitor and a video recorder on a plinth. Apart from some pot plants, the room is empty except for a series of large framed coloured photographs on the wall of some very familiar looking household objects: a jug kettle, a calculator, a garden spade and fork, a plastic child's toy of some description and an electric drill. There are one or two others you have no time to take in before a surprisingly young man walks into the room and introduces himself as one of the partners.

After exchanging pleasantries you explain the object of your visit. Would he be able to help you to design your invention for you? Yes, of course he would – no problem. He clearly rather likes it. But what exactly do you want him to do? Have you got any sketch drawings to show him? You explain rather apologetically that you have not. He counters your contrition with a confident reassurance; that is his job and he would be happy to work up some drawings for you to illustrate your idea as he understands it, in a variety of forms. You are surprised that he offers to do more than one, but he assures you that he already has various alternatives in his mind that he would like to develop for himself.

Finally he comes to the question of fees. You are somewhat taken aback that he charges £80 an hour, but he assures you that his designers are very productive and it will only take them a few hours to create a series of computer-rendered sketch ideas using their up-to-date computer-aided design equipment. You thank him profusely and drive home with your head spinning.

Now you get the picture

Before long you are back at the design studio once again. The same young man is sitting in front of six large colour illustrations on plain white A3 paper. He passes them over to you. You draw in a deep breath – they look wonderful. In your fondest daydreams you had never imagined anything quite like this. You are amazed at how well he has interpreted your sketchy proposals. This feature here, for instance, you would never have thought of *that*... And, in general, he has got it exactly right. It is precisely what you had tried to visualise in your mind all along. He has translated your ideas to perfection.

You get down to business and start to discuss the benefits of this design over that, this feature over another. An improvement here, a variation there, a slight modification to overcome a possible manufacturing difficulty... You are astonished at the designer's understanding of the technicalities; he's already way ahead of you. But it is your idea; he has just used his professional skills to interpret it for you. Finally, after an hour and a half you settle on a single design incorporating a number of features from the other proposals. He says he will work it up into a single finished perspective drawing and call you back when it is ready. You go away with a feeling of euphoria – you are beginning to enjoy your new role as an inventor.

Ten days later you are back in the studio. In the meantime you have called your patent agent and told him what is going on. You thank him for his introduction. He tells you he awaits impatiently to see the results. This time your young designer has a single drawing to show you. It takes your breath away; it is everything you had ever dreamed it would be, and beautifully executed. You find it hard to fault, but the designer does not. He points out that he is unhappy about this, unsure about that, unclear at this stage as to how well this element might work. Nevertheless in general terms he seems satisfied and tells you again what a good idea he thinks it is. Have you done anything more about the patent? he asks. You describe briefly the last conversation you had with your patent agent. The designer pauses and then surprises you: you should not apply for a patent yet, he advises; he still needs to resolve some technical problems if the thing is going to be made to work properly. Besides, it is not necessary; so long as it remains in-house, it is not at all in the public domain; you have yet to disclose anything, your idea is safe with him.

This is beginning to cost you money, albeit entirely manageable so far. But if you want to see this thing through, it is clearly going to cost you a good deal more. You decide to take stock for a few days and reflect on it. You now possess a computerised perspective drawing which illustrates your idea to perfection, but the designer has told you he needs to make a scale model if you want him to resolve the design in every detail and consider how best to make it work. It's a cost that's worth thinking about carefully

For richer, for Broker...

One evening you recall vaguely an article you read in the newspaper some time ago about someone who called himself an invention broker. What exactly is an invention broker? you wonder. The next day you call your patent agent. Has he ever heard of an invention broker? Yes, of course he has, he's heard of several, although he has never had dealings with any of them. Would you like him to look up their numbers? You thank him and await his return call. You prepare yourself this time to tell him you have decided not to file for a patent just yet in the light of your designer's advice. Yes, he says, it is true; so long as you do not talk to anybody about it, apart from your family and trusted friends, and most certainly refrain from showing the drawing to anyone, then the idea remains confidential and exclusive to you. However, he warns you sternly that you must be careful; any loose talk may jeopardise your chances of getting a patent. You may inadvertently lose your claim to your intellectual property rights.

You call the first company on your shortlist of invention brokers. You tell them you have an idea that you are working on but it is not yet patented. Can you come and talk to them about it? Yes, of course you can, but firstly they will send you their standard confidential disclosure document which they would ask you to complete and sign and return to them. In this way you will be protected when discussing your invention with them. The next day the form arrives in the post and you duly complete and return it. A few days later, you get a call inviting you to their offices in central London to discuss your idea. They ask if you have anything to show them – a model, a drawing, anything to illustrate your proposal. You explain that you have had some work done by a design consultant and that you have a colour perspective drawing of your invention. They seem surprised and delighted and ask you to bring it along.

The offices of the invention broker are impressive. They are well-appointed and consist of a number of rooms with busy-looking staff. On the walls are articles from magazines and cuttings from newspapers. Most have a photograph of an individual holding some sort of model or product in front of them and mentioning the name of your broker in the text. It all looks very professional.

The broker comes into the small consulting room and introduces himself. He asks to see your drawing and is visibly impressed. He asked how you came by the idea in the first place and what you intend to do with it. You explain that for the moment you are unsure, you are still feeling your way step by step. He congratulates you on your caution and enthuses over your drawing. He tells you he thinks he can find a manufacturer for you to make it under licence and pay you a royalty. You ask how much the royalty is likely to be and are disappointed when he tells you around 5 per cent, perhaps less. He reassures you that this is quite respectable and explains that it is 5 per cent of the wholesale, ex-works price that you would be getting. He also says that he would probably be able to negotiate a fairly substantial introductory fee of several thousand pounds from the manufacturer to be set against any future royalties. You ask him about his fees and he outlines his terms.

A one-off payment of a substantial sum together with a fixed percentage of the royalties on a sliding scale. The more you pay him up front, the smaller the percentage of the royalties he will take once he has negotiated the deal. You thank him and take away his literature. You prudently decide to allow yourself time to think about it. There are two other brokers on your patent agent's list that you have not yet called. One of them is out of town. You phone them both up and come to the point. What are their terms for brokering your invention? You are surprised by their answers. Neither wants a consultancy fee of any consequence and both explain that they work mainly on contingency. If they can place your invention with a suitable manufacturer they would want a realistic percentage of the revenue. On reflection, this seems to be entirely reasonable; basically a no cure, no fee situation. You decide to visit them both.

Meanwhile, your mind has been working on ways to advance your invention. Are you going to go for a model from your product designer? So far his work has been exemplary; it would be too bad not take the next step. You call him up and give him the go-ahead even though you know that this is beginning to get serious.

Serious money

The designer tells you he is going to develop your idea in two stages. He proposes first to make a scale model of your invention that does not actually work but realises his design drawing in three dimensions. This will enable him to direct his attention onto it more clearly and focus on any technical problems that may arise, particularly with regard to manufacturing. As ever, he sounds reassuringly confident and you feel pleased with your decision. At last the great day arrives when you go to view the model. It is an exciting moment. For the first time you can see your brainchild in a form that can be fully appreciated. It can be picked up, examined, turned over and discussed in detail. You have come to expect a high quality of workmanship; but really, this looks just like the real thing! If only you could just turn it on and make it work... The designer explains he has made a small modification here to overcome a problem he had not foreseen when working with the drawings. He tells you he has a good idea now how best it can be developed. He certainly seems very confident about it all.

And so are you. This is beginning to get somewhere. But the next stage is expensive: a fully working prototype. Are you sure you are ready for that? Where will it all end? Maybe a manufacturer will take it up. Certainly you should have something pretty impressive to show them. You decide to go for it. After all, you reason, once you have a fully working model you will really have something to sell. Nothing is more convincing than a prototype that speaks for itself. The prospect of having the actual product to demonstrate to a potential licensee is compelling

The final working prototype is everything you hoped it would be; the designer has done you proud. The money you have paid him has clearly been well spent. The result is impressive, functional and glamorous – a long way from your own hazy notions of the concept when you first thought of the idea. He is clearly as pleased as you are and wishes you well with it.

Time for a patent

All along you have kept your patent agent informed of developments. You now proudly take your model along to show him. He congratulates you on your professional approach but advises you it is now time to apply for a patent. You have no reason to disagree with him. It is clear you are now going to be showing your invention to everyone and it is time you had some formal protection. Because of the prototype, it is easy for your patent agent to draft an accurate specification with detailed drawings to illustrate it.

Once the specification of your invention has been filed at the Patent Office you are free to show it to anyone. Whether or not your patent will eventually be granted some years ahead remains to be seen. But in the meantime you have your all-important filing date which from now on will remain the day from which you can claim your priority rights to your invention.

But what to do with this wonderful model that you now possess? It is time to take it to your chosen invention broker and see what he thinks. You have already signed a letter of confidential disclosure with him but by now it is superfluous. You have your patent application to protect you. However, he does ask you to sign another document. One in which you agree to pay him a 20 per cent share of the ongoing royalties, should he find a manufacturing licensee for your product and broker a lucrative agreement. Then, suddenly you are struck by a serious problem you had not thought of before. You only have one model! What if a manufacturer wants to keep it, to try out for a while? The prospect of leaving your precious model with a single manufacturer for weeks on end is not something you are willing to accept. Already, the model is out of your hands; it is with your broker. You phone him and explain your dilemma. He assures you that he will not leave it with anybody without your permission. Nevertheless, you feel unhappy about the situation. There are people out there that you would like to show it to yourself; even a possible manufacturer that you personally have come into contact with.

There is only one sensible compromise: you cannot afford to have other models made; what you want is a studio photograph illustrating your invention to good effect, together with a printed leaflet describing it in some detail – how it works and what it is designed to do. At least these can be mailed out. If anyone then expresses a serious interest you can visit them with your prototype and demonstrate it personally. However, they will have to show exceptional enthusiasm to persuade you to leave it with them.

In fact, this scheme works well. Together with your covering letter on your purpose-designed letterhead, your professional-looking leaflet creates a very good impression. You receive several positive enquiries and you feel confident that sooner or later a suitable licensee can be found. You visit a few of them and are encouraged by their interest; they really do seem to think that your invention is a good idea. But they all want to keep the model – it is somewhat embarrassing. Eventually you select one to leave it with in the hope that you have made the right choice.

Awaiting the outcome

After six weeks your patience is running out; and, after ten, you decide to demand your model back. You have been on to your selected company several times and each time they have made encouraging noises, together with promises that they will have a decision for you in a week or ten days at the most. Weeks have come and gone and still no decision – you feel thoroughly frustrated. Besides, there are now a number of other people who are impatient to see it.

You begin the whole process over again. It is starting to take up too much of your time and your regular job is suffering. Travelling around the country visiting people on speculative missions was fun to start with but the novelty has begun to wear off. Your invention broker seems to be somewhat less involved and your wife is becoming more and more fretful. You start to feel genuine unease about the whole situation and wonder why you ever got into it in the first place? The prospect of licensing your brainchild seems to be slowly slipping away.

Then one day, quite by chance, you spot an advertisement in your daily newspaper about a national invention competition. You have never heard of it before – the Toshiba 'Year of Invention'(sadly, no longer running!). You send off for an application form. The competition is divided into six regions around the country and covers various types of inventor. You clearly fall into the independent category. There seems to be no restriction on the sort of invention you can enter, other than the fact that it must not yet be in commercial production. You fill up the form and send it off. Soon after, you receive confirmation of your application and a timetable indicating when the judging will take place and the names of the finalists announced. The months go by and you all-but forget about it. Then one day, out of the blue, you receive a phone call to say that you are one of the two semi-finalists in your particular category in your region and can the judges come and visit you?

The appointed day arrives and two judges turn up at your home to examine your invention at first hand. They are most impressed. They keep telling you how exceptional it is for them to see such a fully-finished invention, one with all its problems resolved in the form of a perfectly designed, fully working prototype. It would appear that you are in with a very good chance. Soon after you learn you have won your category in your locality and are now up against six other independent inventors across the country. You are sent a sum of money and asked to make a video. At last, you are beginning to enjoy your invention once again.

In the meantime, something else has happened: for the first time, you have got some publicity in your local newspaper. The editor heard that you had become a finalist in the competition and sent around a reporter and photographer to write up your story. The subsequent recognition you received from friends and neighbours was all very gratifying. You felt somehow you had finally achieved something worthwhile and enjoyed the acclaim while it lasted. Having made the video, you are now invited to a gala dinner as the guest of Toshiba to learn who will become the overall winner in your category. The big night arrives and for the first time you sense your wife is really rather excited about it all. She has not been on at you quite so much lately, she has clearly become rather proud of you and your invention.

The Master of Ceremonies calls on the director of Toshiba UK to announce the prizes. You hold your breath. Your hands are sweating. You never thought it would come to this. And then the next thing you know you are up on the podium shaking hands with Toshiba's director and clutching a trophy and a cheque for a substantial sum of money, while the photographers jostle for position to take your picture. It is all a bit overwhelming. Out of the 4,000 entries for this year's competition you have become one of the four actual winners, or rather your invention has.

The next morning you lie awake pondering your triumph. Suddenly the phone rings and it is the public relations agent of Toshiba wanting you to do an interview for a national newspaper. She also asks whether you would like to appear on your local radio station as a guest in their popular morning phone-in programme. And that's not all. Shortly afterwards, a manufacturer calls you – one you have never heard of before – who wants to see your invention. He sounds very positive indeed.

'We love your idea... we just hate to try it'

There is no doubt that winning this competition has put your idea on the map. Everybody is now just so enthusiastic about your invention, it seems the whole world wants one and you begin to believe that perhaps you really are onto something after all. Your invention broker calls you also and tells you he has found a couple of new people – one from America – who are most keen to see it. You wonder ruefully just how keen.

So, once again the old round begins; and, once again, you fall into the same trap. After a while you part with your precious prototype and await the interminable deliberations of a new manufacturer. Why can't they make up their minds more quickly? After all it was they who got in touch with you; surely they would have not done so in the first place unless they had carefully considered their interest in the idea? What are they *waiting* for? What else do they need to know? The prototype works. The need has been recognised. The costs have been calculated. After six weeks you decided to put in one final frustrated phone call. You get onto the managing director. (You have met him previously on a couple of occasions.) He is friendly, jovial even, but will not come to the point. You press him, explaining that you plan to come up to collect your prototype tomorrow unless he can give you a good reason why you should not. Then suddenly he comes out with it. He loves your idea; he thinks its great; he would put it into production tomorrow if he could; but the fact is that he really hasn't had time to consider it at all. For the past month he has been negotiating to sell his whole company to a big European corporation.

You hit the roof, and then you collapse into a chair completely drained. It is now fourteen months since you filed your original patent application and recently you paid your patent agent a further £3,000 for an 18-month extension before examination through the Patent Cooperation Treaty. And now this, let down by a manufacturer once again. It's more than you can take. That's it, no more manufacturers, you tell yourself. You have become totally exasperated by your lack of control in these situations and living forever on hope and promises. From now on you are going to do the thing yourself. You are not going to dance to the tune of some mythical licensee ever again.

You let the whole thing rest for a while and give yourself time to reflect, but gradually you come round to the idea once more. Where do you go from here? What assets do you have? A fully working prototype of a marvellous invention that everyone seems to want, but no manufacturer will take up. A patent application taking its measured course towards examination and hopefully a grant, and a search which confirms that at least your idea is apparently novel. Forget the Toshiba competition – it was wonderful while it lasted and the money went to pay for your patent agent's fees, but once the hype and publicity had died down it counted for very little. However, it has had one good effect, it has completely convinced you that your idea really is worth something. And one other good thing: you still have a reasonable amount of money that you can afford to invest in your invention.

Pick yourself up – start all over again

Little by little the old enthusiasm begins to return. In your heart you know you are going to do something about this invention of yours. But deep down you are uneasy about the implications; you know for sure you can no longer play at this. If you are going to do it, you are going to have to do it properly. You are going to have to be professional; you are going to have to become a professional inventor. It is at once an exciting and a daunting prospect.

You start to read books, mainly on marketing. You have no experience in marketing, or management for that matter. The shelves in your local book shop are full of such books. It is hard to make a choice. Some of them look rather dry and are full of charts, clearly written by experts for experts. However, one or two do have compelling titles – *The Complete Entrepreneur*, *Big Ideas For Small Businesses*, *Niche Marketing*, *The Marketing Toolkit* – and suddenly, yes, *Marketing Your Invention*. They all have something to tell you. One or two are very good, but the last one is especially illuminating. You start making notes of the best ideas. Your wife is getting tetchy again.

One day you make a decision. You are going to have a market research report done on your invention. Just as you did with the patent search to confirm the novelty of your product, you are going to do a market survey to establish its commerciality. As it happens, you know of someone in the business and he agrees to do it for you at a favourable rate. It will still not be cheap but, as he assures you, the results will tell you even more than you need to know.

The researcher suggests that he conducts a series of four group discussions with potential users of your invention. Eight consumers are recruited to attend each of the discussions, which are held in a special research studio where you can watch the proceedings from behind a two-way mirror. The studio also videotapes the discussions so that you and the researcher have a complete record of events.

The consumers sit in the studio with your researcher, who guides the discussion around topics which you and he had previously agreed. He covers a lot of ground before he even mentions your idea. He learns what products consumers currently use to do the job which yours is designed to do so much better. He discovers that most consumers do indeed frequently have annoying problems with existing products – the very problems which your device is designed to solve. He gets consumers to describe the features of their 'ideal invention to solve these problems'. Some of their suggestions are uncannily close to your own idea.

At last the researcher gets round to your invention. He shows the photograph of it first, to see how consumers react to its appearance alone. Then he shows some alternative descriptions of its uses and features. These he calls 'concept boards', which help him decide which marketing approach might be best. Finally, he produces your prototype and you can watch consumers try it out for the first time, hear their enthusiastic comments, and note one or two minor criticisms.

Just before the consumers leave, after an hour and a half of intense debate, the researcher asks them to fill in a short self-completion questionnaire. He has designed this to help consumers summarise their overall reactions to your invention, compared with products they currently use. This helps to quantify the results from the relatively small sample, although your friend has assured you that results from even four discussions (thirty-two consumers in all) can be pretty reliable because of the wealth of qualitative data he has collected. Even so, this exercise has cost some £4,500 and it could easily have cost you twice that much had he conducted a more comprehensive survey.

Within a few days the researcher produces his report. The report describes in detail how and why the research was carried out. Key findings are drawn from the discussions and illustrated with quotations which really clarify the consumer's reactions. The conclusions section includes recommendations on the best marketing platform for your product, and on pricing and packaging. The statistical section of the report shows all the written ratings which consumers have given your invention against existing products. A photograph of your invention and copies of the concept boards, topics covered and questionnaire are all appended. Anyone who reads the report should be able to grasp very quickly what your invention is designed to do, and how it has performed in this, its first consumer survey.

The idea works... well, nearly

The results of the survey are illuminating and more than encouraging. They confirm beyond all reasonable doubt that your invention has commercial potential. It has scored above-average on almost every point and has done especially well on perceived value. Almost everybody agreed that they would willingly pay more for it than in fact you would need to sell it for. Your friend assures you that this is a huge marketing advantage.

Armed with your report you go and see your bank manager. As it happens, up till now, you have not talked to him about any of this. You have been with your bank for years but really have never had occasion to get to know him. Your account has always been in credit and you have never had to borrow money. He greets you pleasantly and invites you into his office. You have brought your invention along with you. You show him what it is and explain how it works. You give him the market research report and he glances through it quickly. You explain that you have filed for a patent. You nearly forget to tell him about winning the Toshiba Year of Invention Award last year. He is clearly impressed. He asks you what you want. You tell him you want a line of credit up to £15,000. He seems unmoved. "Could you secure it?" he asks. Well yes, you could take out a second mortgage on the house. He smiles and then asks you a surprising question: "Are you really sure you are ready for this?" It is rhetorical: yes, you can have your loan, but he will want it repaid within three years.

You go home a little punch-drunk – you know exactly what you are going to do now. You are going to put your invention into production yourself. Imagine it, after all these years, you really are going to go off the rails just as your wife had feared. You tell her about your meeting with the bank. You explain you are going to have use the house as security. It is not a good moment. However, you reassure her with a promise that you are not going to give up your job.

The next morning you wake up with cold feet. No, your duvet hasn't slipped off, but your mind has... What do you know about manufacturing? You know you are going to have to get some moulding tools made to mould the components. You know it must be assembled and you know it has to be packaged. A quick calculation suggests a spend of £15,000 before you have even got the first product into a box, let alone a minimum run of five thousand units. Where's it all going to come from? Perhaps you should have asked the bank manager for more – but no, there has got to be a personal limit to this venture. What you're going to have to do is to find yourself a partner. Another investor in the enterprise. Your mind goes blank.

For several days you think about what options are open to you. You have decided for sure that you are not going to go ahead unless a suitable partner can be found. You think about advertising for one in the newspaper, perhaps the *Financial Times*, but it seems all too speculative. Who knows who might respond and how are you ever going to make a selection anyway? You are talking about a marriage here. Would you really want to look for a marriage partner through the classified columns of a singles magazine? Well, you tell yourself, some people do.

But this thought triggers another. There are agencies that arrange these things – introduction agencies, modern business 'marriage' bureaux. They are far more discreet and some are very good indeed. They vet you very carefully before taking you onto their books. The same applies to all their clients. They give you and your prospective partner the opportunity to learn something about one another before introducing you. In fact, wasn't there someone in the office once who found their future partner through just such an agency?

To have and to hold...

The prospect of looking for a business partner through a head-hunting agency suddenly seems to make good sense. You ring your patent agent once again; he seems to be the fount of all knowledge in these matters. Yes, he has heard of such a thing, but knows of none himself. He suggests you call your invention broker. You do. Yes, indeed, he knows exactly what you want. What you are looking for is a business angel and Lucius Cary at *Venture Capital Report* can probably locate one for you.

By appointment, you meet Cary one afternoon in his pleasant offices out at Henley-on-Thames (the company is now based in Oxford). You tell him the whole story of your invention and show him the working model you have brought along. He is suitably impressed. You explain what you want and tell him that you have arranged a line of credit with your bank which, as yet, you have not even touched. You are surprised by his congratulations. He explains how many people he sees who are drowning in debt and desperate to find someone to rescue them. You get on well; you like his enthusiasm. He understands your problem intuitively. He shows you the current monthly edition of *Venture Capital Report*.

In it are about ten articles, each running to four or five pages, outlining the capital requirements of entrepreneurs who have a product or service they want to exploit. In most cases they are seeking expansion capital to fund development plans for an existing business. But in one instance an inventor is looking for start-up money to put his idea into production. You learn from Cary that you have on average a one in ten chance of finding the partner you are looking for through *VCR*.

You look somewhat crestfallen, but Cary is quick to reassure you. Your product is one of the better ideas he has seen for some time and he has one or two of his subscribers in mind who might be very interested in considering it. He outlines his terms for including a report about you and your invention in the next edition of *VCR* and invites you to go away and think about

A week later you are back on the phone to Lucius Cary, having decided to take up his offer. After all, you reason, having determined

58

to develop your invention yourself, you must take the next obvious step. A report describing your idea in *VCR* would seem a modest price to pay for what could lead you forward into a business venture. You are invited out to his offices once again for a formal interview and assessment of your business plan. You remind him that you have not in fact got a business plan. It is not a problem. You are asked to bring along a portrait photograph of yourself and a picture of your invention if you have one. If not, they can arrange to have one taken for you.

Now it's you on the line

At the *VCR* offices you are interviewed by the marketing director. He wants a CV of your professional career and a detailed description of your invention and how it is designed to work. He also needs to know what you require by way of an investment. He questions you closely as to why you think your invention is an improvement on existing products on the market. You show him the market research report that you had commissioned. Finally he suggests that the amount that you are asking for is too low and that you should double it. He points out that an investor may well argue the case for a smaller investment and that your requirements are very modest by most standards.

The following month the article appears in *VCR* and runs to four pages; it looks very impressive. It is a clear synopsis of your requirements and describes your invention in some detail. It contains a small chart outlining the expenditure required to put your idea into production. Your name and address appear at the end of the article, so that potential business angels can contact you directly. There is now nothing more that you can do but wait.

About ten days later, you receive a call from *VCR*. A potential investor has come forward. Cary gives you the details and says he will ask him to call you. Shortly after, you receive a call from a man who says he likes the idea of your invention and would like to come and visit you. You arrange to meet together to show him your prototype. At the meeting he says he has some experience of working with another product which, although serving a different purpose, was in some ways quite similar. He asks if he can take the model away with him to examine it in more detail. Rather apologetically, you refuse. You explain that it is the only one you have and tell him some of the experiences you have had with manufacturers. He says he understands and agrees to get back to you. He goes away having failed to convince you of any serious intent on his part. A few days later he phones up and tells you that, on reflection, he has decided against it.

You hope another investor will materialise, but after a further three weeks you are forced to admit that it is now unlikely. You call Cary in a state of some despondency. You had secretly placed more hope in this exercise than you had realised. After a short conversation in which Cary commiserates with you, he says he thinks he might be able to help you in another way. His next sentence catches you completely by surprise.

Would you like a modest investment from his own Seed Capital Fund? He has been thinking about your invention since you showed it to him, and realises it requires only a small sum to put it into production. He is convinced that properly marketed it could be a great success. He offers you £15,000 for twenty two per cent of the equity of any company you set up to develop it. He goes on to explain how, in conjunction with *Venture Capital Report,* he manages a mini- venture capital fund which specialises in backing start-ups of innovative products that he considers commercially attractive. You thank him, but point out that you have not got a company yet and what you are looking for is a partner with money – a business angel who would be ready to set up in business with you and with whom you could work to develop the product and commercialise it. You feel your own business experience is inadequate, although you believe you might have a part to play as the marketing director of such a company. You need someone with proven business skills.

Cary remains buoyant. As it happens, he knows a company in Bristol that specialises in executive recruitment – headhunters as he calls them. He has reason to believe that they could help. Certainly they have a large network of contacts and have worked in the past with innovator/entrepreneurs in putting together a creative team to start up a business based on an original product idea. He recommends you go and see them.

On the appointed day you meet one of the senior directors at their offices in Bristol and explain your requirements. He is sympathetic and enthusiastic and tells you he is sure they can help. He has recently been engaged in an assignment to put together a team to exploit a new product from America that an entrepreneur had discovered over there and got exclusive rights to market in the United Kingdom. As far as he knows the company is now up and running and doing very well. He seems to think your situation is not dissimilar. He offers you his literature and outlines his terms of business. You go away feeling heartened by the meeting.

A few weeks later you are called to their offices once again to meet a man perhaps six or seven years your junior. He is smartly dressed in a blue suit and wearing a red tie. He shakes your hand confidently. He details his qualifications, which include a degree from the London School of Economics, and goes on to outline his experience in business. It is impressive. It seems he has been in manufacturing most of his working life and has recently been the managing director of two small companies which he bought a share in, turned around and sold at a profit. He describes himself laughingly as a company doctor. He is now looking for a new opportunity, something a little different from his previous ventures, in which he can enhance his entrepreneurial abilities and add to his overall experience. He likes the idea of your invention very much and, what is more, he has some money of his own he would like to put into it.

Love at second bite

Over a series of informal meetings you begin to get to know your potential new partner; you like him more and more. He is a straight talker and clearly ambitious; he knows where he wants to go. He outlines his scenario for your invention. He suggests drawing up a business plan. He is confident that the product can be developed in stages and the risks minimised throughout. He seems to have a clear understanding of the problems that may lie ahead. He suggests that the first step is to set up a limited company with himself as the managing director and you as the marketing director. He agrees to invest £10,000 of his own money in the company in exchange for twenty per cent of the equity. This means that, together with Seed Capital's investment of £15,000 for twenty two per cent, you still retain fifty eight per cent of the company. For the £10,000 you have already put into it yourself and the £15,000 loan you have arranged with your bank, the company is effectively capitalised at £50,000, making the value of your own equity in it already worth more than your actual investment.

One of the things he particularly likes about your invention is what he calls its 'theatrical qualities'. You had always been aware that it was an exciting and impressive product to demonstrate but had never considered this to be a particular asset. Your new partner assures you that from a marketing point of view it is a big bonus. Once the company has been incorporated, the first thing to do is to set up a small office with all the required equipment: a computer, fax and answerphone and a secretary who can take calls, keep the accounts and run the office. A single room with a couple of desks is perfectly adequate. In the meantime, you must find a contract manufacturer to make your product and a graphic designer to design the packaging for it.

Fortunately, because your invention has been so well designed from a technical point of view by your original product designer, it is relatively simple to make and assemble. You approach a number of contract plastic moulders and get some comparative quotes. You decide not to go with the cheapest, but rather with the moulder who offers to assemble the product for you as well. The tooling costs will take up £25,000 of your available capital and the balance will go on the first batch of five thousand units.

This in effect would leave you without any working capital at all. Before committing yourselves to tooling you talk it over with your partner. He confirms from Seed Capital that they are unwilling to increase their investment at this stage and from you that you are unable to borrow any more money from the bank. After some deliberation he agrees to put in a further £10,000 of his own money in exchange for another ten per cent of the equity. You are not altogether happy with this as it reduces your share in the company to less than half – forty eight per cent – but really you have no choice, and the value of your shares has not been effectively diminished. Once all this has been agreed and settled you instruct the moulder to start making the tools; they are going to take between ten to twelve weeks to complete. There is little more you can do now but to get yourselves and your new company set up in an office. Your partner agrees to take on this responsibility, allowing you to stay on in your job for another few months. It is clear, however, that the time is fast approaching when you are going to have to resign your position and devote yourself full-time to your new venture.

Tooling up for business

Another thing you can do while waiting for the tools to be made is to get the packaging for your product sorted out. You appoint a graphic designer to come up with some alternative proposals, bound by the need to have a box with a display window to show the product inside, and a hole at the top to hook it onto dispenser rods inside retail outlets. He also designs some simple, coloured A4 sales leaflets illustrating your invention.

At last the long-awaited day arrives when your tools have been completed and the first moulded components have come off the machine. You visit the local trading estate where your moulder occupies one of the factory units to examine the first production samples of your product. It is a tremendously exciting moment when you hold the first fully-manufactured example of your invention in your hands for the first time. Your brainchild has finally been born. You have brought along some of the packaging boxes that have already been made and try the product out inside one of them. It looks exactly as your designer had illustrated.

At last, the day arrives to give up your old job; it is both a terrifying and an exhilarating moment. But you have had so long to prepare for it that you do not hesitate – you have broken out at last. Your wife is now resigned to the inevitable (and really rather proud of you); she is going to support you all that she can.

The following weeks are a whirlwind of activity – you have never worked so hard in your life, but it's all tremendously exciting. You arrange a press release with your local newspaper, which first broke the story about your invention back when you won the Toshiba 'Year of Invention' award. The story that now appears is very flattering.

Your next job is to visit all the independent shops in your area that might be interested in stocking your product. Most people are aware of it through the two pieces that have already appeared in the local paper. They know you are the inventor and they are keen to try it out with their customers. You have no difficulty in selling a few samples to each shop. You provide them with copies of your literature in a special unit that they can display on their sales counters.

Meanwhile your partner has been busy thinking ahead; in two months' time there is the annual trade fair of DIY products at the National Exhibition Centre. He has reserved a small stand in the main hall and has been arranging for posters and literature to be printed up for it. A special display stand will have to be made to show off your product to best advantage. In no time at all it seems that the date is upon you and you prepare to spend four days in Birmingham. The response from visitors to the fair is tremendously encouraging. Several of the buyers from the big retail trading companies express an interest and a couple of buyers from Germany place significant orders. They tell you that they expect to see you at the big international trade fair in Cologne early next year.

By the end of the fair you count up the orders and realise you are going to have to run your single-impression tools twenty four hours a day if you are going to meet your delivery dates. Maybe the time has come to consider commissioning another set of tools. Your partner is already making enquiries about having sets of multiple-impression tools made out in the Far East. The difference in price for both the tools and the moulded parts is dramatic. Less than a third of the price you are paying in the United Kingdom.

Sunday special

One day you receive a surprise call from a company called Innovations. They have become aware of your product and would like to sell it through their mail order catalogues. When you get home and tell your wife, she goes to a drawer and pulls out a small A5 size illustrated catalogue. She tells you it arrived with the Sunday papers some weeks ago. There are one or two things in it that she rather fancies. You examine it with interest. Every page has four or five photographs of consumer products together with a small caption describing them. The catalogue contains a whole host of innovative new ideas. There must be more than three hundred of them altogether. You are vaguely aware of having seen a sample of it in the past, but now your attention is much more focused on it. It would seem a wonderful way of getting your invention into mail order. The following month your product appears in the pages of the catalogue, *The Innovations Report*. The sale price is more expensive than it is in the shops but still entirely reasonable in terms of value for money. In the coming weeks you receive a constant stream of orders from Innovations which takes up almost the whole of your production capacity. It is definitely time to commission another set of tools. Your partner contacts the agent he has been dealing with with regard to manufacturing in China, and for a fraction of the price of making the tools in England he commissions a set of four-impression tools with an option to be increased to eight impressions if required. In a couple of months you will have multiplied your manufacturing capability by a factor of five.

On the strength of your growing sales, your bank manager has agreed to double his lending limit to you provided you regularly meet his monthly interest repayments. Your cash flow is very healthy, but the increased capital allows you to pay for the new tools in China.

One day your partner has a surprise for you. He tells you that without letting you know he took your invention to the producer of *Tomorrow's World* at the BBC in London and they have agreed to demonstrate it live on tonight's programme. You chide him good-humouredly for not having told you before, but he says he wanted to surprise you and besides, had he told you earlier, you might both have been disappointed if nothing had come of it. That night you stay at home with your wife and watch the programme with eager anticipation. You have no idea what to expect. The presenter announces at the beginning that they have an item on your invention later in the programme. When it comes around it lasts no more than three minutes, but the demonstrator does it all beautifully, making the most of its theatrical properties in a very entertaining manner and highlighting its best features most effectively. You are thankful he has got it so right considering it was a live presentation. You feel a warm glow of satisfaction and your wife is clearly impressed.

Tomorrow, the world...

The following day, *Tomorrow's World* phone you with a whole list of enquiries they have received as a result of the broadcast. Many are clearly from potential end-users, but a sprinkling are from retail buyers all over the country. It seems you are going to have to expand your marketing efforts and perhaps take on some national sales assistants as well.

But perhaps the best outcome of the TV showing is that one of the big national DIY companies places an order with you for a dozen products to be stocked in every one of their retail outlets throughout the country. It is a huge order, and you are thankful that the delivery date is almost due for your first consignment of products from China. With luck you will be able to meet their deadline for delivery in two months' time.

Another unexpected result of the *Tomorrow's World* programme is that the producer has invited you to enter your invention in the Prince of Wales Award. He refers you to Business in the Community, the organisation that administers the award, and they send you an application form. It is now December; you have until the end of January to get your application in, but it needs to be completed in some detail. In April you learn that your invention has been selected as one of the six finalists for this year's competition and will be featured on the last programme in the current series in June, when you will be invited to meet Prince Charles at Highgrove House and present your invention to him personally.

The eagerly-awaited day finally arrives and you and your partner present yourselves smartly dressed at Highgrove to meet the *Tomorrow's World* team. The filming takes two days and Prince Charles is present throughout to talk to the contestants. Finally the winner is announced on camera. It is not you – you are the runner-up. The programme is screened the following week.

Your partner is determined to make the most of this considerable achievement. He contacts a small public relations company he knows asking them to generate as much publicity out of your success as they can. In the next two weeks you are interviewed by seven reporters – three from the national press, two from women's magazines and two from general interest DIY magazines. You also appear again on your local radio station. One of the best stories to appear as a result of all of this is a feature in the *Financial Times*, which publishes a long article in their small business section about how you came upon your idea and how you have since managed to develop a business around it. The gist of the story is by way of illustrating how a good invention should be exploited. The article clearly applauds your acumen.

The following month there also appears a two-page feature in the colour supplement of one of the quality Sunday newspapers, showing you standing next to your smiling wife in the garden of your home, holding up your invention and looking somewhat smug. (Your friends tease you about it.) The story is written from your personal point of view and tells how you took the gamble and gave up your job to develop your own invention. It concludes by saying you will probably end up very rich!

We have ways to make you rich

Around about this time you receive an update call from your invention broker, Pax Technology. Over the years they have kept in regular touch with you while promoting your invention through their international network of manufacturing contacts. John Emanuel, the managing director, tells you how delighted he is with your recent triumphs. He saw the Prince of Wales Award on television and also the colour supplement article. He has his own good news for you. One of the original manufacturers that he has been in contact with since the beginning of your venture has recently got back to him and expressed an interest in licensing in your idea. When you ask him which one, it turns out to be one of the biggest manufacturers of domestic appliances in Germany, who have a high market profile in the United Kingdom. He asks if you would like him to set up a meeting at their London office to meet the managing director. You discuss it with your partner and agree.

The following week, all three of you arrive at the well appointed head offices of the German company. You are treated with some ceremony, almost as VIPs. At the meeting there are several other senior directors present. You get down to business. They explain that they have examined and tested your product in detail and decided that they would like to license the intellectual property from you, now that your patent has been granted. They will not discuss their terms at this stage, but only ask if you would be interested. When you press them on the sort of terms they have in mind, they reiterate that this would be a matter for a later discussion, once you had agreed in principle. The only thing they do emphasise is that they would like worldwide exclusivity and go on to point out that they have a major presence in 63 countries around the world.

After the meeting you go back to Pax Technology's offices to talk it over. It certainly seems an attractive proposal, and John Emanuel clarifies what it all means in real terms. He says first of all that he should be able to negotiate the licence agreement for you if you wish and get a first-class deal out of the company. He assures you he has a great deal of experience in these matters. He reviews the terms of the agreement you have with him and makes a modest concession of two and a half per cent to his existing percentage in the light of your own skilful and successful development of the product. He says it has made all the difference to his own efforts on your behalf. He congratulates you both on a splendid achievement.

You go away and talk it over with your partner. You have been together in your company for over three years now and have got on well enough. But you sense that if things got very much bigger, your relationship with him might become strained; you really are two very different people. Your partner says that from his point of view it all depends on the best overall deal that John Emanuel can negotiate with the company. You decide to agree to Pax Technology's proposals to open negotiations with them.

The whole process takes a surprisingly long time, but in the end you are completely satisfied. The German company agrees to buy all your tools and stock from you at the market price. They also agree to take a licence under your patent for a down payment of £30,000 and a six per cent royalty on sales with a guaranteed minimum income in the first five years of £25,000 a year. They tell you that they are confident that once they are able to distribute your product internationally, which will take about two years to achieve, you and your associates can expect royalties of well over £100,000 a year. Your partner, who now owns thirty per cent of the company, seems quite satisfied with this and Lucius Cary of Seed Capital Fund is delighted. His £15,000 investment for twenty five per cent of the company has proved particularly lucrative. However, you must take into account John Emanuel's seventeen and a half per cent, negotiated with you down from twenty per cent, which reduces all your equity pro rata. Nevertheless, this leaves you with almost forty per cent of the company. If the licensee's predicted sales of your invention are realised, you can look forward to a personal royalty payment of around £40,000 a year and all you will need to do in principle is to pay the annual patent renewal fees which, at this early stage in the life of the patent, remain extremely modest.

You recline in the glow of your success and wonder why the gods chose to smile on you. Another time, you might not be so lucky. But then, there's never going to be another time – is there?

5

The Fallacy of the Patent

To the uninitiated, inventions and patents are almost synonymous –
the two would appear to go hand in hand. Everyone knows the word
'patent' and that it is closely associated with inventions. They have
heard of patent agents and the Patent Office, but to the credulous
inventor it is a hazy picture. Few are aware of the procedures or the
prohibitive costs involved. But a powerful aura surrounds the patent;
the possession of one somehow implies a passport to riches.

With his mind inflamed by such fantasies, the first-time inventor
enters the arena. Before long, someone suggests he apply for a patent.
It is taken as a kind of compliment; an idea worthy of a patent must
surely possess some authentic merit. The proposal appears to validate
his invention. It takes little to persuade him to file for one. But first of
all he must find an agent. It is not difficult; they are widely dispersed
throughout the country. His new-found agent is unlikely to quell his
ardour. Only if his invention is truly far-fetched is he liable to be dis-
couraged. The patent agent's job is to draft specifications and file
applications for their clients and process them professionally towards
grant. He will examine your invention's patentability, but he is
unlikely to express an opinion as to its commerciality.

Invariably, the innocent inventor becomes the proud owner of a premature patent application. His agent is not to blame; he has carried out his client's instructions. But our hapless inventor is unaware of the floodgates he has opened. Patent applications have a life of their own; in no time they begin to assume the status of intellectual property with an insatiable appetite for money. If they are not nourished by due dates, they die; they cannot be resuscitated. Your fledgling patent can all too quickly turn into a voracious monster devouring your money. However, a fully-granted patent is not without teeth; provided the inventor has been persuaded not to file his application too early, and encouraged initially to concentrate his efforts on developing his idea further, the time may come when a patent application appears a far-sighted investment.

Heads we win...

A patent is a form of insurance. The patent agent is your insurance broker and the County Court your claims assessor. Unfortunately, the Patent Office is not the insurance company but merely the keeper of the records. If only it were, recompense for proven infringement might become a foregone conclusion. If someone steals your car, provided the insurance company is satisfied of the fact, they will pay up – there is no argument. If someone steals your invention, the argument can go on for ever and cost you a fortune in legal fees. In most cases taking your case to court is just not worth it. There is no certainty that you will win and even if you do there is no guarantee you will be paid. A patent is a form of insurance that the impecunious inventor may sensibly decide to go without.

The purpose of a patent is to act as a deterrent. It is your only legal remedy against plagiarism, but in reality patents do not prevent inventions from being stolen. If your product is successful it will soon be copied, you can depend on it. The thief knows he is unlikely to have to face you in court. He gambles on your being unable or unwilling to prosecute your claim to your intellectual property. In most cases he is right. He is able to steal your idea from under your nose and walk away with two fingers in the air. It happens all the time.

So what's the purpose of a patent if it is so easily violated? Is it a paper tiger? Ron Hickman, who invented the Workmate, would be the first to disagree. The intellectual property invested in his patents earned him a considerable fortune. Although he licensed the idea to Black & Decker, he retained the intellectual property in his invention. Throughout the life of his patents he brought and won many actions against infringers from all over the world. Every time he won, the strength of his patents was increased. Even though the cost of all this litigation was prodigious, the royalties he earned from this single licensee over the years far outstripped it. His patents were quite literally his passport to riches.

So where's the contradiction? In fact there is none. Ron Hickman was in a position to uphold his patent rights through the courts only because he had already licensed his Workmate to Black & Decker. Had he not done so and was still making it himself, it is likely he would not have been able to afford the crushing costs of litigation. Had one infringer been seen to get away with it, others would soon have followed. Filing for a patent and pursuing it to grant is one thing; defending your rights to it under law is entirely another. To patent or not to patent? – no question is more fundamental to the inventor. In fact, the decision should rest on only one consideration: that you are more likely to make money with a patent than without one. In most cases you are not.

Judge Ford and the Patents County Court

For many years one of the most daunting prospects faced by any inventor in pursuing an alleged infringer of his intellectual property, was the high cost of proceedings in the High Court. Its legal procedures were protracted, contentious and horrendously expensive. Indeed, unless he was rich or had patent protection insurance, it was invariably beyond his means. This encouraged anybody to trespass on his patent rights with impunity knowing full well they had little to fear from the law.

In recognition of this predicament, a White Paper was published by the Government in 1986 which explored ways of making patent litigation cheaper and more accessible. Following this, a committee was formed under the chairmanship of Sir Derek Oulton QC, which concluded that jurisdiction should be conferred on special County Courts, charged with hearing all types of cases regarding intellectual property. The court set up to be the first Patents County Court in the UK was at the Law Courts in Wood Green, North London and was inaugurated in September 1990. The judge appointed to preside was Judge Peter Ford who had previously worked for many years on the Board of Appeal of the European Patent Office in Munich.

The principal difference between a case heard in the Patents County Court as opposed to the High Court, is in the procedures leading up to it. Whereas in the High Court it is presumed that the case will come to trial, in the Patents County Court everything is designed to prevent that. The procedure employed is the Preliminary Consideration. Here the two disputing parties are asked to put their case to the judge informally in his chambers. Judge Ford will have received all written pleadings well in advance of this meeting and will have acquainted himself with the facts in the case. It is here that he will encourage the two parties to resolve their differences. He will also express his own views as to the legal position which can only help to clarify the arguments and often leads to settlements out of court.

Another great benefit of the Patents County Court is that solicitors and patent agents are free to represent their clients instead of barristers. This tempers the atmosphere of the whole proceedings and saves hugely on costs. The plaintiff has only to pay the fees of his advocate during the hearing, as all the Court's costs are met by the State. Of course if he wins, he may be awarded his costs against the defendant, or vice versa. In certain circumstances, when he is clearly impecunious, he can apply for, and even be granted, Legal Aid.

On those occasions when a case does come to a formal hearing, it has been so thoroughly aired in advance, that the trial rarely takes more than a few days before the judge is asked to adjudicate. So far the formula has proved hugely successful and more and more litigations regarding intellectual property are being dealt with by the new Court. To date it is coping well with the workload, but should this trend continue, it is possible that other regional courts may be appointed as Patent County Courts to localise and extend the service throughout the country.

In moto perpetuo

If you can accept from the outset that really you are a hobby inventor, then in truth you should not patent at all. It is a needless waste of money. Even if you file only in the United Kingdom and eventually go on to get a patent granted, in practice it is pointless. You keep going round in circles. Like patent agents, the Patent Office has no business deciding if your patent application describes an invention with commercial value. Its only remit is to accredit novelty. If you apply for a patent on a new form of spaceship, it will probably be granted. The shelves of the Patent Library are littered with such nonsenses. The only thing they will reject, regardless of novelty, is a perpetual motion machine on the grounds that it defies the laws of physics. No examiner is qualified to say whether or not your spaceship will fly; the assumption is that it might and therefore on the basis of novelty you are entitled to protect it.

You should not only avoid the cost of applying for a patent on your crankier creations; sometimes, even sound consumer inventions are better off without one. The cost of pursuing a patent all the way through examination to grant is substantial. Using the services of a patent agent to draft your specification and process the application, even in the United Kingdom alone, will cost you up to £1,000. Once you start to file in other countries in Europe and around the world, that thousand pounds will multiply many times over. For the average inventor it is dead money. For the reality is this: if your product does not sell either to a licensee or through self-production, your patent is worthless, it has nothing of value to protect. And even if well marketed, unless your invention is so exceptional as to become a world beater and a classic in its own right, its chances of recovering its investment in patent fees remains highly unlikely. Assessing the true earning power of your idea is imperative.

The difference between a patent applied for and a patent granted is enormous; the distinction is often not well understood. The former is merely a masquerade, the latter a lethal weapon. The patent pending is no more than a speculation, but the patent granted is a persuasive deterrent to any would-be infringer, so long as he knows that you have the will and the power to enforce it. However, anyone wishing to acquire a fully-granted patent had better consider his bank balance. Securing a portfolio of international patent rights requires a very impressive capital commitment from any inventor.

Call my bluff...

In spite of their temerity, patent applications do have their place. Few go on to full grant for one of two reasons: either they are abandoned by their applicants or they are rejected by the examiner. The former is by far the most common. To get a full patent grant can take up to four years and cost substantial sums of money; most inventors wisely decide to forego the expense. The cost of an application on the other hand is negligible, particularly if you are able to file it yourself. You are not obliged to use the services of a patent agent to draft your specification, and the act of filing is simple enough. If you do not intend to go for full grant, then this is a sound ploy for it has one important advantage: a patent applied for entitles you to print 'patent pending' on your product.

Everyone has seen the term 'patent pending' inscribed on a plastic-moulded product. The Patent Office now disowns the term because it somehow implies that it is only a matter of time before the patent will be granted. Nothing could be further from the truth. In many cases it merely acts as a decoy. People put 'patent pending' on products that carry the flimsiest of applications. But before twelve months are up, the applicant must decide if he really wants to take the next step and keep his application alive, at least up to publication. This involves paying £130 for a preliminary search of prior art, after which an abstract of your invention will be published in the *Official Journal of Patents* eighteen months after your original filing date.

Until publication the competition has no way of knowing if you have made a serious application or not. It is a strategic ploy, for by this time you should be well ahead in the game. If your filing date coincides with the launch of your product, you can give yourself a head start of up to two years, and with the 'fashionable' type of inventions this can be more than enough.

What sort of inventions merit this ploy? The best candidates are those with a limited life span. Nowadays we live in a 'global village' when it comes to marketing. It is entirely possible to distribute a new product all over the world in a matter of months. If you are lucky enough to hit upon a novel idea that could create a craze for only a year or two then a patent is pointless – for, by the time it is granted, you should have walked away with your winnings, leaving your competitors to pick up the pieces. There is nothing to be gained by pursuing them, for by now you should be well on your way with your next world-beating invention.

Another good example is an invention that may have a limited market but is relatively easy and inexpensive to produce; something where tooling costs are low and even modest sales produce a profit. If it is successful it will be copied, but that very success will continue to generate sales for your own product. If it fails, you will not have wasted your money.

It's all in the timing

When it comes to patenting, timing is everything. The conventional wisdom is that you should patent as early possible; for the average invention the reverse is the case. The argument goes that someone may be working on a very similar idea to your own and that your filing date is your only legal claim to priority. This may be true, but in effect it generally applies only to technological inventions. Very often research establishments are working on corresponding projects; state of the art decrees it. In a race to be first, every new development becomes the subject of a patent application and it is only when the dust has settled and the technology formerly unveiled that the various competitors can discover who has won the race. It is not necessarily the first to have finished, but the first to have patented it. This is not the natural domain of the independent inventor.

It stands to reason, therefore, that if you are not going to patent as early as possible, then you should leave it as late as you can. A patent agent will tell you you cannot disclose your invention and apply for a patent thereafter. Actually that is not quite correct, you can file for a patent after public disclosure – there is no law against it, and the Patent Office will be none the wiser. Only when an infringer proves that your invention was in the public domain prior to your filing date is your patent invalidated. In order to be successful your adversary has to pin down a date: he saw it in a particular exhibition, on television or in a magazine article before the date of your application. He has to furnish irrefutable evidence. It is no good his saying only that a friend of yours whom you had shown it to told him about it in a pub about a month or so before you patented it. He is going to find that impossible to prove.

Keep it under your hat...

In fact, there are a number of forms of disclosure and they need to be examined here in some detail.

First there is **confidential disclosure**. This in itself has two distinctions: automatic and authorised. Automatic confidential disclosure is when you talk to somebody about your invention who is bound by professional ethics to hold the information in confidence. Many of the organisations mentioned in the section on 'Help for the Inventor' fall into this category – namely, the innovation centres, the enterprise agencies, the design consultants and, of course, all patent agents. With these people your secrets are safe automatically.

I am inclined to add competitions as well; however, here you must be more careful. All competition entry forms advise you to apply for a patent before entering and state that the organisers will take no responsibility for the consequences if you don't. In this they are right; naturally they must protect themselves. But in fact they tend to be very good about keeping all information in confidence until the time has come to declare the winners. These, of course, have to be announced, but you will be informed of the fact in advance. The best course of action is this: prepare an application in anticipation of winning but do not file before you know the outcome. Once drawn up it can be filed immediately. The majority of the contestants will never reach this stage and their inventions will not be disclosed in this manner. For most of the entrants it will be far too early to apply for a patent and unless you are amongst the finalists it will prove premature.

When it comes to **authorised disclosure**, the procedures are formalised, but the effect is the same. When showing your invention to a manufacturer it is prudent to ask him to sign a letter of confidentiality prior to the presentation. The larger companies are disinclined to do this; but, as explained earlier, there is little point in showing them a product in prototype form in any event; they are so unlikely to buy it. But with the medium to smaller companies, they can usually be persuaded to do so.

Your typewritten 'letter of confidentiality' (which should be presented on a single sheet of paper, in duplicate, and contain no more than two or three paragraphs – a standard form is available from The Chartered Society of Designers, price £7.50 + VAT) should be tendered as a prelude to the meeting. They will have no time to think about it and will look conniving and untrustworthy if they refuse to sign it. You offer it to them as a standard routine formality. They can hardly argue with that.

Once signed you are protected. Although not a legal document in itself, such a letter would convince any court of its purpose and would invariably be upheld in your favour. But more importantly it becomes a statement of intent by the company. No company would be foolish enough to attempt to steal your idea once such a letter was signed and stored in their files. It would be more than their good name was worth. The letter of confidentiality is a simple and powerful document which is often underestimated. It certainly rules out your need to make a patent application prior to such a meeting. However, it must be said, any reputable company would not contemplate stealing your idea under such circumstances, letter or no letter, so the risk all round is negligible. You only become vulnerable when your invention is in production and on the market. If you have not got a patent filed or granted by then, you are fair game for all.

The other two forms of disclosure are **private** and **public disclosure**. They are not nearly so well defined. Private disclosure is when you show a relative, a friend or even a colleague in assumed confidence. You can always tell them to keep quiet about it, but normally it is not necessary – the trust is implied. The chances that this sort of disclosure will lead you to losing your rights in your invention are remote, but there is a thin dividing line between private and loose talk and you must be wary of it. For instance, you might show it to a private gathering of work colleagues, some of whom you hardly know, and then wonder why a patent application for a similar product is filed in an unfamiliar name soon after the event.

Public disclosure is, as it implies, the exact opposite. Once a description or photograph of your product has appeared in the newspaper or a magazine, on television or on the radio and most certainly been seen at any sort of trade fair, it is in the public domain; there is no question about it. If you have not yet filed your patent application it is legitimately too late; it has become public property. Anyone can take it up with impunity and although unable to file for a patent on it themselves they can commercialise the idea in any way they want.

However, remember what was said earlier; you can apply for a patent after public disclosure and very often get away with it. For example, your invention could go onto the market and become a great success. Suppose a company in America that has no knowledge of the history of your invention decides to infringe your patent and put the idea into production themselves without your permission. If you then defend your rights in your intellectual property (assuming that your patent has now been granted) and the only argument that the infringer can raise against it is on the grounds of novelty, you may still win your case. However, it must be said that this is a risky course of action and few inventors would allow themselves to slip into the precarious position of filing after the fact.

Ideas in limbo

Although this chapter may appear to denigrate the value of the patent, I have tried only to clarify some of the misconceptions that surround it. The patent is invariably upheld as a hugely desirable asset, whereas so often it is much more an expensive liability. More intellectual property has been lost through premature patenting than ever was through untimely disclosure. The reason is simple: the patentee can no longer afford to keep his patent extant while his invention remains in development and shows no signs of generating an income. During the first year of a patent's life a request for preliminary examination must be made and the full fee paid to the Patent Office. If this is not done within the statutory twelve months, the application automatically lapses and the patent falls into the public domain. Here it may languish in a sort of limbo, for once an invention becomes public property no manufacturer is likely to be interested in it unless they are convinced of its exceptional commerciality.

Always remember that a patent is 'intellectual property'; it is not just some fanciful abstraction – its assets are tangible. Its true worth lies in its ability to make money. Unless real money can be generated by exploiting it, it will hold little benefit either to its owner or to a third party. The more money your invention can make, the more valuable are your rights to it, and the more you can build its ability to make money, the more valuable your patent becomes. Every inventor dreams of one day selling his intellectual property, but all-too often he finds there is no market for it. Before committing yourself to the cost of acquiring a patent, ask yourself clearly just how you intend to exploit it. No question is more central to the business of invention.

Making money out of intellectual property must qualify as just about the most difficult enterprise any inventor can undertake. For only by adding value to his patent does he create something to sell. As we have seen, he can do it himself (as did our inventor in 'Growing Your Own Invention'), but he may find another most unlikely ally in his endeavours – one which his patent is wholly designed to protect him from – a thief, a blatant infringer of his intellectual property.

The ultimate deterrent...

It is possible to take out patent protection insurance (PPI) against the cost of litigation in the event of infringement of your intellectual property. Its value is debatable because it will not be invoked unless your case is incontrovertible. With the recent inauguration of the Patents County Court, the cost of such litigation has been greatly reduced, making it easier for the individual to meet the costs. As a deterrent however it is very valuable. For a modest premium an inventor can buy £500,000 worth of legal fees in the United Kingdom, which is not a sum a cynical infringer can casually ignore.

PPI can add real muscle to your patent and an infringer can inadvertently add value to your intellectual property. For if you take him to court and win, your patent is strengthened, no doubt about it. Looked at another way, an infringer is a licensee without a licence. He is enhancing your invention both commercially and financially. He is creating an awareness and a demand for it in markets other than your own. All you want from him is a small portion of his income, the right to your legitimate royalties. If you allow him to become well-established and committed to your invention, you may well be able to come to a lucrative agreement with him without recourse to the law. And, if he is convinced you can win your case against him, you can make him an offer he can't refuse. You would end up with substantial compensation and a considerable windfall in backdated royalties, making real money out of your idea.

At the heart of every serious invention is a patent – the two certainly do go hand in hand. But what the inventor needs to decide is whether he really wants one. A patent is a powerful tool when attached to a good invention, but a mediocre invention will find its weight unbearable, incapable of recovering the money invested in it. A patent is a form of insurance, but some ideas are just not worth insuring. An invention is a product of the imagination. A good inventor can conjure up ideas in his head almost at will. In amongst them there may be one or two that could create a fortune; the others are mostly just toys. He should enjoy playing with them for the pleasure alone.

PART TWO

Sources of help for
inventors

Introduction

Since the turn of the decade the impression has grown that innovation has overtaken design as the fashionable panacea for all the industrial ills of this country. Of course this is not the case, but for the moment innovation is in the ascendant, acknowledged even by the DTI through its Innovation Unit. There has never been a better time to be a British inventor.

The following chapters provide a reference map for the inventor. The aim is to help you assess, develop and exploit your idea in the most judicious way possible by describing the network of expertise that is available to assist you. It lists nine different categories of help that the inventor can turn to, illustrating the various alternatives through which an invention might be developed. You must decide for yourself what options are most relevant to your idea, and consider to what extent you are prepared to commit yourself. Even with the best-laid plans, there is never any guarantee of success. No business activity is less likely to make money; the inventor must keep a tight rein on himself if he is to avoid being completely carried away with his idea.

Don't get carried away – or you <u>might</u> be!

A common problem facing the inventor is over-enthusiasm. It is inclined to colour his thinking. The very act of creating something new is so intoxicating that he is inclined to lose sight of reality. He searches for a solution to his conundrum and when it comes, often unexpectedly, it is an exhilarating moment. He senses he is trail-blazing, and in a sense he is; but whether his particular trail is worth blazing in commercial terms is another matter.

The underlying theme of this book is the quest for success. It is the legitimate raison d'être of the inventor. If you do not seek to make money out of your invention then you are a hobby inventor and so be it – there is nothing whatever wrong with that. However, if pursuing technical solutions to theoretical problems is your pastime and pleasure then you have no business with the Patent Office, or indeed most of the other organisations described in this section, although a visit to your local Business Link might be instructive.

For the practical inventor things have never looked better. There is now an extensive, and often dedicated, network of help available to assist you. Its emergence is relatively recent and in many cases no more than a few years old. If you have the makings of a good commercial idea, now is the time to try to exploit it. But it is important to get some third-party commitment to your idea; you should never attempt to go it alone.

There is an old cliché that might have been coined for inventors – 'fifty per cent of something is better than a hundred per cent of nothing'. The inventor would do well to remember it. Countless inventors have failed by trying to hold on to too much for too long. The correlative of that is they spend too much too soon. Almost everybody has a little money to invest in their invention; the important thing is to invest it wisely, little by little, as it is required. Without doubt one of the best ways to go about it is to share your investment with somebody else – two minds are better than one, and two bank balances are far better than one, especially when your partner's is much bigger than your own.

Whatever you do, avoid borrowing excessive personal sums from your local bank manager. It is a delusion to think you will be able to pay it back quickly – you will not. Nothing is more protracted than the commercial exploitation of an invention. Being saddled with a compounding debt at high interest rates is the daylight nightmare of far too many inventors; it should be avoided at all costs. The encouraging thing is, it often can be.

Spread the risk

The importance of finding a partner cannot be stressed too strongly; it is by far the best way to nurture success. A partner can take many forms. For instance, some inventions can only be licensed to a company. If this is the case then your only practical partner is an invention broker. His job is to try to license your product to manufacturing industry. If he is successful, the partnership will have been a fruitful one.

In another instance, your ideal partner might be a design consultant. If your chosen designer is prepared to put your invention through his own innovation company and take equity as a fee, it is an offer the inventor would do well to consider. The chances of success become so dramatically improved that almost any equity exchange is well worthwhile. Inventors are notoriously reluctant to give away equity but often pursue a licence agreement as if it were the holy grail. The best you can expect from a licence agreement is around five per cent, but with a joint venture agreement you may well do very much better.

Then there are the options of venture capital and business angels. These are appropriate only for the entrepreneurial inventor. Most inventors are not entrepreneurs by nature and even those who are, are invariably committed to some other professional activity. Setting up an enterprise to exploit a new product is a serious business and you must be certain you want to take on the risks and the responsibilities. But if you do, find yourself a partner who will make his own investment in your venture. Provided you can work together and establish a practical division of labour, you stand a good chance of success.

Another word of advice – try not to be too precious about your invention. If you have come up with one idea, you can be sure there is another waiting just around the corner and very often the next is better than the last. Professional inventors are often prolific creators. Sometimes their output is prodigious; with a few they succeed, but with most they fail. Sir Clive Sinclair is a classic example, for whatever the commercial outcome of his latest brainchild, he always has his inventing 'eye' firmly fixed on his next fantastic vision of the future.

The only thing you need to remember at all times is this – do not allow yourself to run out of money. Once that happens you are done for. Of all your resources, money is the most valuable – and finite; be sure to spend it with due deliberation.

1

Public Sector Support

As is customary in this country, it takes private enterprise to inaugurate an intiative which when proven successful is taken up by government and relaunched in its own image. Thus it is that the independent Innovations Advisor sponsored by BP in the early 1990's evolved into the government-appointed Technology and Innovation Advisors seconded to the modern Business Link bureaux which are now located throughout the country.

A first consultation with an Innovation Advisor at a Business Link is free and confidential. The inventor can, of course, use this advice at his own discretion, but he will generally find that referrals from a Business Link to other organisations and companies within the network carry with them considerable credibility.

One of the most difficult tasks faced by the Innovation Advisor is gently to persuade and enthusiastic inventor that his idea is not worth pursuing. It may be technically impressive but commercially inadequate for sime reason. The advisor's conclusion may be open to question, but his reasoning will be objective and should be considered carefully by the inventor before he proceeds. An originator is often so enamoured of his offspring that as time goes by he is increasingly inclined to turn a deaf ear to sound advice and may simply throw more good money after bas. This situation is so common as to be regarded almost as a syndrome. So take care. Take good advice from good advisors; they really do have your best interests at heart and can save you a lot of toil and tears in the long run.

Another profitable source of advice and assistance for the innovator are the Business and Innovation Centres to be found around the country situated in Business Parks. Here the aspiring inventor will find at his disposal a communal workplace equipped with good, basic engineering facilities and staffed by excellent technicians,where he can effectively design, build and market his product all under one roof and at the same time rub shoulders with like-minded compatriots in the business of invention. The Centres are renowned as effective networkers in their local communities and have extensive connections with manufacturing industry. They can even help complete an application for a SMART award which is beyond the capacity of most individuals unacquainted with its rogorous requirements.

Business Links

A government White Paper on education and training in the late 1980s resulted in the setting up of a network of local training and enterprise councils (TECs) to structure Britain's approach to training and enterprise development. The first TECs came into being with the new decade, and over the past few years have joined with Chambers of Commerce and Regional Enterprise Boards all over the country to create a chain of **Business Link** organisations, housing under one roof all of the country's main regional business support infrastructure, freeing the TEC s to concentrate on sponsoring training initiatives, and offering (in many cases) basic communal facilities; including a business library displaying a wide range of relevant publications, market research and mailing lists (beware of these, they may be anything up to six years old and so, by now, ninety per cent inaccurate!), training and meeting areas and casual workspaces with phones, copiers and faxes available.

Business Links are funded by the DTI and the Scottish, Northern

Ireland and Welsh offices, and provide a range of advice and training services to small businesses and start-ups. They are a valuable source of information about any grants that may be available regionally.

Virtually all Business Links now provide a standardised service for innovators, run by a full-time Technology and Innovation adviser. The 'small business' innovator is made aware of any grants that may be available to him. In addition, he is also directed towards possible sources of professional help. Ultimately, if an idea 'clicks', he may be introduced to firms in the area with similar products, if any. As one Director put it: "The service is designed to bring inventors in from the cold and give them reassurance that someone really does care about their idea and will do all they can to encourage and help them."

In addition, most Business Links now offer a package of support measures, including free counselling, up to four days' free training (delivered by private consultancies on contract to the TECs) to develop your business skills – plus a small cash grant on completion. If you are unemployed, please note that this could affect your benefit entitlement.

Business & Innovation Centres

A number of regional Business and Innovation Centres (BICs) belong to the European Business & Innovation Network, based in Brussels. Local authorities in regions that have been designated as having special development needs may seek support from the European Commission to set up a Business and Innovation Centre. Initially support may be at fifty per cent of eligible costs for up to thirty months. The remainder of the funding comes from the local authority and the private sector. Leading companies such as British Steel and British Coal Enterprise commonly make contributions. Many of these Centres have gone on to develop themselves as standalone businesses, thriving on a mixture of public and private sector funding. Details of four of particular interest are set out below.

Barnsley Business and Innovation

Among such centres nationally, the Barnsley Business & Innovation Centre in South Yorkshire benefits in this way. Established on a greenfield site on the outskirts of Barnsley, it consists of a number of incubator units which the entrepreneur can rent at subsidised rates. Although there are no communal workshop facilities, the Centre provides a team of professional advisers whose assistance can be sought at any time. The advisers address such matters as product appraisal, business planning, marketing, prototyping, patenting and fund raising. The purpose is to provide the technical innovator who has entrepreneurial abilities with the opportunity to set himself up in business.

Manufacturing & Technology Unit, Nottingham

The Manufacturing and Technology Unit at the Lenton Business Centre in Nottingham provides a role model of what an Innovation Centre should be. It was set up ten years ago as a joint venture between Nottingham City Council and central government with a view to promoting employment and business growth in the region.

The Centre's operations are broadly divided into two areas. The first provides a service for inventors who can use the facilities and expertise of the centre to assess the technical and commercial viability of their ideas and carry them forward into design prototypes. Provided with a well-equipped workshop for model making purposes, the Centre also offers advice and assistance in such areas as engineering design and technical drawing and sourcing of materials, and can advise on things like patent searches and regional government grants. In a number of cases it has been instrumental in helping its clients to achieve a SMART award through the DTI.

The second service the Centre offers is to entrepreneurs (often qualified engineers who have been made redundant), who decide to set themselves up in business by renting a unit within the Lenton Business Centre. By allowing these individuals to use all the services of the Centre at reduced rates, Nottingham's new unitary authority effectively subsidises the development of fledgling companies to the point where they can become independent, with the objective of creating new jobs in the community.

SCEPTRE (Sheffield Innovation Centre)

An offshoot of Hallam University, based on the next-door Sheffield Science Park, SCEPTRE stands for the Sheffield Centre for Product Development and Technical Resources. The Centre is solely dedicated to providing a comprehensive range of professional services to small and medium-sized businesses. Product and process innovation are supported by prototype manufacture and 'hands-on' technological and commercial consultancy.

Run by Tony Marsh, SCEPTRE offers a fully-equipped, on-site prototyping workshop facility, providing over 200 square metres of floorspace. The workshop comes with a wide range of wood-and metal-working machinery, in addition to equipment for forming and fabricating plastics. A full-time team of specialists are on hand, with considerable international experience and expertise in design engineering, materials handling and product development. A project management service is offered, as are the vital support functions of sales and marketing. These services are used by inventors and businesses from all over the UK.

Initial consultations with SCEPTRE are free: and many of SCEPTRE's services can also be provided free to clients located within the Objective 2 areas of the Yorkshire and Humber region, with EC support. Because SCEPTRE is administered by the University's world-famous Engineering department, which is close-by, clients have ready access to state-of-the-art CAD and other facilities for modelling and analysing engineering proposals. In addition, Tony Marsh points out, there is the extensive academic resource of the University to draw on when problems need to be solved.

Businesses and individual inventors have three main routes into SCEPTRE: the first being free, 'self-drive' use under the Innovation Skills Development Programme (ISDP). This training development

93

scheme, mainly for young and unemployed engineers, is only available to clients within the Objective 2 area more-or-less covering South Yorkshire, and meets all the client's costs and expenses, including travel. Inventors who are competent engineers but who do not qualifyfor ISDP can also have 'self-drive' access to the prototyping machinery at a subsidised rate of £7 an hour. Finally, the full resource can be used on a commercial basis by company clients, who pay an agreed fee to work with SCEPTRE's own staff to design and manufacture a functional prototype. This latter route can also be used for small off-line batch or test production runs, enabling the company to continue manufacturing using its own facilities.

SCEPTRE works closely with Business Links and other organisations in supporting proposals with possible commercial potential. Its consultants, says Tony Marsh, are committed to innovation, and: "To enabling our clients to introduce profitable change and maintain a competitive edge." To this end, SCEPTRE will research and identify market opportunities and look for appropriate transferable technologies to allow businesses to branch out into new markets. Tony Marsh is convinced that SCEPTRE's unique appeal is based on its business networking strengths, its access to research facilities and its ability to provide up-to-date advice and technical support from concept, right through to market.

North East Innovation Centre Ltd

Based in Gateshead, the North East Innovation Centre covers the North East region and has close links with the other providers of technology and business support in the area. Since its inception in 1980, the Centre has evolved far beyond the original concept of Innovation Centres, which were primarily concerned with individuals and product ideas. It provides technological support to all comers and most of its activity is concerned with the design, development and manufacture of production machinery and equipment for manufacturing firms – including some of the largest in the North East.

George Ord, the Centre's Chief Executive, explains: "The North

East Innovation Centre provides a regional service, both to individuals with new product ideas and to companies with a need to develop or improve their product, process or production machinery."

The Centre is strongly market-orientated, and its technical staff have visited ninety per cent of manufacturing industry throughout the region – almost six thousand companies – to find out what kind of technical support they need. Ord points out that the vast majority of small firms want practical, 'hardware' solutions to real manufacturing problems. The innovative application of tried and trusted technologies, coupled with progressive improvements, minimises or eliminates the risk and high costs associated with the use of 'cutting edge' technology.

The North East Innovation Centre is a non-profit making company limited by guarantee, and funded by local authorities, Business Links, the EC and, increasingly, from income generated by design and manufacture of machinery and automated systems for large companies.

The Centre has twenty four employees comprising mechanical and electronics engineers, workshop technicians and administration. Four business start-up units are available where individuals can develop their product ideas and move into the initial stages of production. Several have gone on to create significant businesses employing up to one hundred people. The Centre also operates a Professional Engineer Development Programme, taking on four engineering graduates each year for on-the-job, fully-paid training.

Scotland

It's certainly true to say that, if you decided to relocate to an area of traditional economic deprivation, you'd get more support as an innovator and entrepreneur now, than it is possible to find in the wealthier areas of the country. Scotland is a good case in point, as there is a remarkable range of schemes available to provide support, advice, contacts, premises and cash for developing new technology-based businesses. The two main bodies responsible for administring these, one private, one public, are:

Scottish Innovation

Founded as the Strathclyde Business & Innovation Centre, the company began winning a number of national contracts in the early 'nineties and with the re-organization of the Strathclyde regional authority changed its name and its remit to include the whole of Scotland. Scottish Innovation is an associate member of the European Business & Innovation Centres Network. It offers a comprehensive service to advise the innovator/entrepreneur in all aspects of setting up and growing a profitable business, and sponsors a major award scheme. A full-time staff is on hand to provide a wide range of consultancy services at highly subsidised rates (up to fifty per cent). It provides an opportunity for a small company with an original product to match the facilities of a far bigger organisation at a fraction of the cost. In other words, it can 'buy in' professional services, as and when required, as an external resource, thus keeping its overheads down and its initiatives effective.

The range of services starts with new product appraisal, through all aspects of business development and staff training, to an ultimate goal of exporting into Europe. A bonus for companies setting up under SI's umbrella is an optional scheme whereby payment for services rendered is deferred until the new product, which may take some time to develop, actually goes into production and starts earning real money. In some cases, equity in the new company is accepted in exchange for fees or else they can be exchanged for royalty payments.

This support package, with its flexible and imaginative options, has enabled many new companies in the region to realise substantial commercial success with their innovative ideas. Scottish Innovation would seem to be a Mecca for an entrepreneur with an original idea, whether it be a product or a service – or even an original marketing plan. It is targeted primarily at entrepreneurs already resident in Scotland, but anyone with a commercial idea who is ready to relocate to the region is welcome.

Scottish Enterprise

Excluding the Highlands and Islands, which is covered by a separate Enterprise board, Scottish Enterprise comprises thirteen areas of the country, administering a hundred and forty separate business development initiatives. Obviously there is not space enough here to cover them all, but a few key ones will suffice. The forty Business Shops, for instance, have an approximate parallel to the Business Link centres in England, being a first point of contact for entrepreneurs to enter the complex system of business support that is available. The Business Forum is a unique idea, enabling entrepreneurs to have their proposals evaluated by a panel of experts. A Small Business Loan Scheme is underwritten with European money, and enables the Scottish clearing banks to make capped loans to approved projects. Scottish Development Finance provides up to £500,000 equity finance for business development in targeted industries, while LINC Scotland arranges more informal equity partnerships. Between them they have around £30 million a year to invest.

The **Glasgow Development Agency** operates an initiative linking business and higher education, to enable technological innovators to 'commercialise' their ideas. Again, support is focused on particular industries, particularly biotechnology, optoelectronics, software development and new materials. Forty eight new companies have been launched under the model Entrepreneurship Programme run by the Lanarkshire Development Agency. A liaison between Strathclyde European Partnership and Glasgow University, 'Targeting Technology' also provides help for entrepreneurs hoping to market their technological inventions.

All in all, over 4,700 new businesses have been created in Scotland with the help of these various schemes; while existing businesses can benefit from the development of numerous science parks and technology exchanges fostered by the area Development Agencies in partnership with the private sector, benefiting from generous relocation allowances. Scottish Enterprise plans to assist a further 2,500 new businesses to come into being by the year 2000 under its 'Business Birthrate Strategy'. It sounds like Scottish independence is in the ascendant.

Northern Ireland

Local Enterprise Development Unit (LEDU)

For as long as anyone cares to remember, Northern Ireland has suffered the ravages of sectarian conflict and has become a byword for social deprivation and economic decline. But although politically the region remains in turmoil, economically the province has benefited enormously from development finance, and from the recent, short-lived ceasefire, which allowed foreign investment to flow into the country. Two key organisations provide an excellent support infrastructure for the revival of business and the encouragement of innovation. They are the Local Enterprise Development Unit (LEDU), and the Industrial Research and Technology Unit (IRTU).

LEDU has its origins in the **Rural Development Commission** over 20 years ago, but, as the big international companies gradually pulled out of the area, so LEDU's role evolved into helping small businesses grow and prosper in their place. Says Bill McGowan, LEDU's development services manager: "It was as if a forest of large mature trees was laid waste and in their stead thousands of seedling enterprises have sprung up that we are helping to nurture into mature companies." In fact, ninety five per cent of all companies in Northern Ireland employ fewer than fifty people.

In the past couple of years, LEDU has inaugurated a number of novel self-help programmes aimed at the innovator/entrepreneur within the small business community and has set up public sector seed capital funds to back them. The most recent of these is the BIL Award, the Business Innovation Link of Northern Ireland. It is effectively a new company, limited by guarantee, and sponsored by LEDU, its parent and prime-mover, together with the Northern Ireland Innovation Programme (NIIP), an offshoot of LEDU, which acts as its treasurer.

Says David Maxwell, LEDU's senior technical adviser: "BIL is an initiative peculiar to Northern Ireland which grew out of a need to re-focus our primary efforts to help grow small businesses in the region. Up until recently we used to give grants to companies for material expansion, such as new machinery or building grants, in an effort to create more jobs in the community, when what we should really have been doing was encouraging competition. So we have re-directed our efforts towards innovation, marketing, training, management skills and so on, nurturing the culture of a company towards enterprise and excellence in all aspects of its business. Although our budget from the Department of Economic Development runs to around £30 million annually, our portfolio consists of four to five thousand companies – which means we must target our resources very carefully."

The BIL account is in fact very small (less than £100,000) but it is unique, at least in the UK, in that it is seed capital provided by the public sector. Administered by NIIP, it provides what every inventor needs who has a gleam in his eye but insufficient funds to turn his brainchild into reality. The award is granted to someone who, in the opinion of a panel of experts, has an idea worth developing.

Although the applicant must match half the grant himself, up to £4,000 is available for product and business development, which can include applying for a patent. If necessary, the money can actually be given in advance rather than retrospectively, which is normal in most grant situations. For the aspiring inventor this can be immensely help-ful. With the money comes a mentor. His or her job is to act as a con-sultant to the inventors and direct them towards the various sources of technical help and professional advice that remain available through LEDU's extensive network of contacts. This ensures that the inventor is spending his own and other people's money to the best effect. Maxwell neatly sums up BIL's objective: "It can help an idea to get over the first hurdle and on to the stage where it can present itself as a credible start-up proposition."

The BIL Award is therefore only a first step in a process that can enable the innovator with some entrepreneurial ability to realise their ambition to start up a business based on their idea. For, after BIL comes **Innovation Equity Ltd.**, NIIP's investment fund and effec-tively BIL's big brother. Innovation Equity is managed much like any other venture capital fund, the big difference being that once again it is public sector seed capital. It is funded by the International Fund for Ireland, a European Community Resource, and supported in part by the Presbyterian Foundation of America, a charitable trust with Irish antecedents. It has resources of around £1 million. Because of its remit to back small business start-ups the fund is able to provide much smaller sums than conventional venture capital groups could or would want to manage – typically between £10,000 and £50,000. For its investment NIIP takes an equity stake of up to forty per cent of the company in ordinary voting shares.

Sally McCole, who is NIIP's business development adviser, is cautiously optimistic about the prospects for the investment fund: "Our task is to assist in the identification, creation and development of innovative technology-based businesses, particularly those with good export potential. The fund has only been operating for about two years and so far we have made twelve investments throughout the region, each one averaging about £30,000. It is far too early to say whether any of them are going to realise a profitable return for us in the five to eight year timetable we are looking at, but if we can eventually show a profit on our investment in that period we shall be very pleased."

TEP, Northern Ireland

Another special programme set up by NIIP is an experimental venture aimed directly at the entrepreneur. Its unique formula is to select five individuals and focus the spotlight on them for fifteen months, offering professional business advice from every practical point of view. It is perhaps the nearest thing to hot-housing a business start-up that has yet been attempted. Says Sally McCole: "So many small businesses fail and very often it is simply due to the inexperience of the individual. Getting going in business is one of the hardest things anyone can do. Our aim is to set someone securely on his feet from the outset and give him every chance of growing a successful business in the long run."

Entitled the Technology Enterprise Programme (TEP), it starts out by selecting eight promising people and marries them up with eight commercially interesting propositions. Of course the entrepreneur may well have an idea of his own which would be looked at very carefully, but there is also an ideas bank in the offing from which the innovator can select any viable idea that appeals to him. Small businesses in the region can also draw on the ideas bank for inspiration.

For the first three months these carefully selected budding entrepreneurs are each given a monthly living allowance of £500 and an additional £400 for market research and development. Certain out-of-pocket expenses can also be met, and for the product itself a development grant of up to £1,000 is available. A 'business godfather' is appointed to offer advice and assistance and keep an eye on progress. After three months the most promising five are chosen to go forward to the main programme of setting themselves up in business.

At this juncture a business grant can be made available from LEDU through BIL (up to £4,000) to get the company going; although by now the entrepreneur would be expected to match this with his own money. But by the time he has been selected for the programme, he will have already received over £3,000 gratis and can still continue to draw a living allowance for a further three months. He can also, if he wishes, apply for an additional low interest personal loan of up to £3,000. Says McCole: "We don't exactly throw money at him as we want him to learn what life is like in the real world. But what we do offer is the opportunity for somebody to get started in a way that no other programme makes possible."

For the next twelve months the business is monitored very carefully and every assistance in the way of free advice and hands-on help is provided, including further technical development money for the product if required. If the innovation that is being created has a technical aspect, a 'technical godfather' is appointed from one of the two Northern Ireland universities to give practical assistance in its development. In fact, a whole team of specialists can be called upon to focus attention on the fledgling company who will do all that they can to set it on its feet. Says McCole: "The objective is to arrive at a point where after fifteen months the business is sufficiently sound to allow the entrepreneur to put together a business plan and approach us at NIIP for an investment from our venture capital fund, Innovation Equity. Considerably larger sums can be made available from this source in exchange for equity in the new company and of course we know the whole history of the company from its conception. If we are satisfied with what has been achieved so far, we are more than likely to look favourably on any further application for investment."

TEP has all the makings of an imaginative and promising experiment which, if successful, could well point the way forward for the rest of the country to grow new and viable businesses into the next century.

Grants

It is commonly supposed that start-up and other grants are readily available to small business entrepreneurs, but this is no longer always the case, particularly outside the economically-deprived areas of the UK. Government policy has been to move away from direct funding of enterprise, to a 'self-help' culture in which accredited bodies are grant-aided to provide a framework of support for applicants, but no actual funding. There is no shortage of advice, and a visit to your Business Link is recommended; but don't be too disappointed if they simply give you the name of a business manager at your local branch of NatWest or Barclays.

Regional Enterprise Grants

The latest news is that these are in the main being subsumed into the DTI's SMART scheme and will have to be competed for (see DTI SMART awards, page 131). However, in one form or another regional entreprise grants will remain available in specific areas earmarked for development (such as those affected by coal and steel closures, for example), funded both at EC and at local government level.

Details may be obtained from Government Offices in the UK regions, or contact your local Business Link.

European grants

In addition to the regional enterprise grants referred to above, there may be alternative types of grant funding available from the EU, depending on the type of project and the precise location. However, EU grants are very difficult to obtain, particularly by individuals, and inventors are not recommended to spend a great deal of time pursuing this line of enquiry. A conversation with your Business Link will confirm the availability of this kind of funding for your particular purposes.

Further information

For further information on all matters relating to the availability of grant funding, the first point of contact, as indicated above, is your local Business Link. A number of Business Links now offer access to **Grantfinder**, a computer database 'trawling' service provided by the firm **Finance for Business**, covering both UK and European grants. If your Business Link can't provide this service, **Gloucestershire Business Link** can; contact Tony Williams on 01452 509560. You will need to be totally specific about the areas of search, and how much money you want to find. There is a £20 fee payable for each search. (Some other Business Links offer a similar service called Ecufinder.)

2

Technology Bureaux and Exchanges

If innovation is the fashion of the 1990s, then technology is its catalyst. The last twenty years have seen huge multi-national companies grown from a single technological breakthrough and economists the world over have urged their governments to back high-tech. Being a small country with no natural resources, the Japanese long ago realised the benefits of adding value to basic materials by transforming them into state-of-the-art technology. Nothing attracts investment more readily than a really high-tech innovation with worldwide potential. Being first in the field with such an idea ensures a monopoly market internationally.

In collaboration with NatWest bank, John Allen has written a book called *Starting a Technology Business*. It outlines some of the ways in which a technological innovator can bring his idea to market. NatWest, as we shall see, has identified technology-based businesses as being a growth area for the future and has focused its attention on supporting them through its Innovation and Growth Unit, run by Duncan Matthews, and a range of locally-and centrally-based services, including the Technology Business Manager Network, Appraisal and 'Business Angels' services.

Essentially it encourages an enterprising entrepreneur to start up in business with capital from NatWest. Without doubt, seed capital is the hardest form of venture funding to find and in the past many good ideas have foundered through lack of it. But if he has the right credentials and a promising product to go with them, an innovator has every chance of persuading the NatWest Bank to back him.

Technology exchanges. on the other hand, enable both the inventor looking for backing and the established business seeking fresh ideas with good commercial potential to come together, initially without any obligation or risk attached.

Increasingly, such services are available on-line, or are published as electronic media; the problem being, as Brian Padgett of The Technology Exchange identifies, that the domain of new ideas and technologies is expanding almost uncontrollably. It is now virtually impossible for any one information provider to keep track of everything that is going on, while new ideas are replacing old ones faster than they can be commercially applied. By and large, technology exchange media are for the serious specialist inventor or University researcher, as the technologies they represent require increasingly sophisticated resources available only to the R&D departments of multinational corporations. However, they are in the main publicly accessible and their increasing sophistication need not preclude them as a fertile source of ideas and contacts, even for the smaller inventor.

NatWest Innovation and Growth Unit

"NatWest is the only bank with an open door policy towards technology businesses. The success of the Innovation and Growth Unit proves that this is what the market wants. We will continue to respond to their needs." With these words, Duncan Matthews, head of the bank's Innovation and Growth Unit, proclaims his wholehearted commitment to new technology businesses. Once upon a time, it could fairly be said that banks, particularly at local branch level, had little understanding of the needs of start-up businesses. In the eight years since the Unit was set up, however, the bank has created a **Technology**

Business Manager Network of over two hundred and sixty branch managers with extensive training in this area. Their rôle is to connect the bank and its customers with the key sources of advice and help that are available.

The specific brief of the Technology Manager is to consider financing requests; supporting these where necessary with a **New Technology Appraisal Report** prepared by an independent technology or marketing consultant with a view to assessing the commercial potential of the project. This allows the Technology Business Manager to reach an objective decision as to its eligibility for funding.

What is expected of the entrepreneur is a professional approach and, in particular, a well-presented business plan. It can be very difficult for an individual applying to his bank as an independent inventor to make any sort of credible impression without some convincing credentials. A referral from a science park or a regional technology centre, particularly when endorsed by the director, will often achieve greater impact. It is essential that the business plan stands up to scrutiny; there is nothing like a bad plan to undermine a potentially good proposal.

In most cases, a package of loan finance can be tailored to the requirements of a business using traditional banking facilities, such as overdrafts and start-up loans, as well as making use of any grants available. In addition, loans can be provided under the **Small Firms Loan Guarantee Scheme**, in which the DTI underwrites a proportion of the loan, minimising risk.

'Business Angels' – individual investors, typically with amounts of around £250,000 to invest in innovative companies – may also be identified and introduced through the **NatWest Angels Service**. Says Duncan Matthews: "The object is to advise entrepreneurs how to get the best out of their inventions and in the process we hope to realise many ventures that would otherwise not get off the ground. At the end of the day, we are looking for entrepreneurs with an ability to start up a business and a promising new idea – it doesn't have to be startlingly original. If the innovation has been nurtured in a science park or comes to us with all the right credentials, it has every chance of finding a business partner in us."

In addition, the Unit publishes a thrice-yearly colour newsletter, *Innovation Business*, giving a wide range of advice on matters of interest to innovative small businesses, such as intellectual property, business planning, technology updates and alternative sources of support. Distribution is free on application.

Technology Exchanges

However an inventor chooses to exploit his idea, provided he has taken sensible steps to protect his intellectual property (which does not necessarily mean taking out a patent, as we have seen) he has something to sell to a third party. An exclusive licence to an international manufacturer with worldwide markets would seem an ideal objective, but such agreements are very rare and are beset with uncertainty. It is far better to grant a sole licence to one or more smaller manufacturers and leave the option open for self-manufacturing. This allows the formidable costs of development and of worldwide patenting and maintenance to be shared, possibly between a number of licensees, and reduces the considerable commercial risks associated with going into production. It also throws the market open to competition, which in almost every case results in increased sales and market growth.

It is easy to find examples, particularly in the computer and electronics industries, where non-exclusive licences have been of unbelievable benefit to the inventor, for instance Dolby noise reduction or Microsoft Windows. Equally, it is possible to point to cases like Apple computers, whose early refusal to license their uniquely user-friendly operating system has lost them substantial market share, despite its technological advantages over the rival PC-DOS system. Information-sharing, provided its commercial exploitation is properly protected in law, has got to be good for everyone.

In one respect, offering intellectual property for sale is no different from any other commodity; it needs to be advertised. This is the function of Technology Exchanges. Subscribing companies are given access to the wealth of new technology contained in their databanks.

It can prove a bountiful supply of fresh ideas for companies acquainted with this resource.

There are very few national databases of new technology in this country which, apart from **BTG**, keep up-to-date records of emerging technology (although since privatisation, BTG have been able to devote only limited resources to researching the ET market, and in any case, never made their data, which was largely client-confidential, publicly available). Much of this shared technology emanates from the research laboratories of academic institutions, but the inventor need not be overawed by this. If he believes he has something to sell which could be of interest to a foreign company, he has little to lose by lodging his idea with an exchange. It could lead to an enquiry with far-reaching consequences.

The Technology Exchange

The Technology Exchange is a technology transfer organisation that disseminates intellectual property data through its *Technoshop Catalogue,* now available on CD-ROM and by fax to subscribers in over fifty countries around the world. Although always open to entries from individuals, most of the Technology Exchange's input data and enquiries come from companies, universities and regional development authorities, particularly enterprise agencies and innovation centres. Increasingly, too, information exchange has been taking place between governments and research institutions in the North, and the developing countries of the Third World.

In fact, the field of technology transfer is changing with unbelievable rapidity. Brian Padgett, Director of The Technology Exchange, describes the effect on his own business thus:

"Since our earlier discussion, we have been forced to make a major change in the way we disseminate information to industry about new intellectual property available for licence, joint venture or outright sale of IPR rights. This has been caused by the huge increase in the number of opportunities and in the number of sources of technological developments with whom we are now in communication and the rapidity, both in turnover of the technology and the ever-shorter lifetimes during which new IPR remains 'state-of-the-art'. We have also found that the demand from industry to identify partners in other countries who are seeking new technology developments and licences for existing, well-proven technology, particularly for the growth economies of the developing countries, is at least as important as the transmission of information on new technology developments for licence.

"We have been working intensively with UNIDO, the World Bank and, more recently, with the European Commission to research the needs of individual enterprises in the developing economies. Since 1991, in co-operation with the Governments of the individual countries concerned, we are now making both technology and partnership requests and international technology offers the subject of a technology and partnership targeting service for industry, which is being delivered via e-mail and fax to subscribers with follow-up introductions at a cost of £40 per month plus VAT."

The Technology Exchange, says Padgett, is co-operating with Hertfordshire Business Link to develop the service in association with the other UK Business Links, as a front-end, 'new business introduction service' which can be provided as an essential reference to Business Link users. This move will simplify delivery of what is reputably one of the best-established and most comprehensive international sources of information and opportunities for joint ventures available, both to inventors seeking to get their products to market, and to companies seeking marketable ideas.

BEST

Building Expertise in Science and Technology (BEST) is a database of technological research and development operated by the publishing group, Cartermill International, and located in St. Andrews, Scotland. Available on CD-ROM, updated twice a year, it is the UK's official database of technological expertise that emerges from British universities, and government research establishments throughout the country. Its role is to disseminate this information to British industry for potential exploitation. BEST is not concerned with the 'small inventor', but is purely an information exchange service. A subsidiary database, Innovations, enables companies to keep track of scientific research into specific processes.

Much of the information is passed to BEST by gatekeepers, the industrial liaison officers within the institutions, whose job it is to interface between the rarefied environments of high academic research and the commercial requirements of industry and the marketplace. Registering state-of-the-art expertise with BEST is an important first step in the process, providing a shop window for academics and their knowledge. Should industry then express an interest in this expertise (after accessing it with an on-line password), BEST can provide a detailed CV from its database and refer the enquirer back to the researcher. It is then up to the parties concerned to pursue the possibilities of a licence agreement, or indeed any other form of marketing exploitation of the intellectual property, for the mutual benefit of the institution and the inventor.

BEST claims to have over forty one thousand records of individual scientists and their activities in the fields of physical sciences, life sciences and engineering innovations stored in its database. To be able to access this valuable resource a company is required to pay a subscription in proportion to the number of users, with a minimum of £3,900 per annum. In addition to the BEST database, Cartermill International publishes a twice-yearly journal called *Innovation* containing brief descriptions of about a hundred new inventions. This is also sent to subscribers for an additional fee of £195. Says Gill Joy, Cartermill's Business Development Manager: "The service we offer facilitates the dissemination of practical information relating to the results of academic research between the interested parties. Without it a dialogue between them might never begin to take place."

The Institute of Patentees and Inventors

Together with a leading regional newspaper group, the Institute of Patentees and Inventors (IPI) has set up a unique 'faxback' service to allow inventors and business entrepreneurs to gain access to a comprehensive nationwide database of inventions. Members of the Institute can apply to join and are then entitled to receive hard copy information about any of the companies or services listed. Under the 'Inventions and Innovations' category, inventors can rapidly obtain up to six pages of lists of manufacturers, distributors, licencees and investors, all of which, claims the Institute, will have been pre-qualified according to their specified area of search.

The Institute is a non-profit making organisation offering its thousand-plus members advice and guidance on all aspects of getting their ideas to market. It sponsors an annual exhibition, the Great British Innovations and Inventions Fair, in London. Discounts on books, seminars, courses and company visits also form part of the membership package. Of especial interest, as it may well be the only such course being run anywhere in the country, is **'Sustainable Invention'**. Held in conjunction with Richmond upon Thames College and the Open College Network, it covers all the procedures and stages of bringing an invention to market. Individual membership of the Institute costs £50 a year, Company and Student membership grades are available.

Footnote

At the time of writing, Gloucestershire Business Link are setting up a unique new information and business opportunity service aimed at innovative small to medium-sized enterprises (SMEs) in the South West region later in 1997. In conjunction with a major international management consultancy, the programme – funded with UK government money – aims to help subscribing companies by providing highly selective technical and scientific information on leading-edge technologies. (Not suitable for backroom inventors!) The success of the programme may stimulate similar schemes at other Business Link bureaux – contact the scheme's innovator, Tony Williams.

3

Design Consultants

No group of professionals is better qualified to help the inventor than Design Consultants. Although sometimes slow to admit it, many of them are very creative inventors in their own right. The imagination of the product designer is not dissimilar to that of the inventor. The difference is only in the professional skills the designer is able to bring to bear.

In my experience any money spent with a design consultant is likely to be an excellent investment. In the first place, they will examine your design proposal very carefully and give you an opinion free of charge. Product designers are used to looking at drawings and models and thinking in three dimensions. The designer will understand your requirements absolutely. He has a natural ability to conceptualise. You may even be surprised at how easily he is able to grasp the technical implications of your design and foresee any future problems. He will intuitively understand what you want.

His instinct is in seeing your idea as a product with market potential; something he is called upon to do every day by manufacturing industry His mind is acutely attuned to the realities of the marketplace. He will know right away whether the invention can be made and for what price and indeed what the competition is, if any. He will appreciate precisely its degree of novelty. At the end of the meeting he will tell you very clearly whether, in his opinion, it is worth pursuing as a commercial venture. No other source of gratuitous advice can be so comprehensive.

All this will give you food for thought. It is meant to. For if you decide to use his services, it will start to cost you money right away. Designers charge by the hour and they do not come cheap. But two or three thousand pounds spent at this stage with a creative designer may prove absolutely invaluable. A source of free advice, most Business Links have a Design Councillor who can provide an initial view as to the viability of your invention.

So what will you get for your money? In all probability a very well thought through, beautifully designed, technically resolved, fully functioning prototype that you can be proud to present to any potential client. Having used the services of a designer, you will have automatically enhanced your credibility and increased your chances of finding a buyer for your idea. In addition, the designer will by now identify closely with the product himself and will be only too pleased to accompany you to meetings that seek to sell it.

In some instances, if he believes strongly enough in the product, he may even agree to waive your portion of his fee in exchange for equity in your invention and a share in any royalties it may eventually go on to earn. It can be an excellent way to realise your brainchild in a resourceful and cost-effective manner.

There are a good many design companies in this country, a product of higher education that offers design studies very widely on the curriculum. It is also the result of the fashion for design in the 1980s when students were attracted to what was seen as a glamorous and rewarding profession. However, since the recession, there has been a shake-down in the industry with many smaller companies going out of business, whilst others have merged and rationalised. But there are still probably more design companies in this country than anywhere else in the world, and the British have an international reputation for design excellence. Students always are always needing work experience, of course, and the resourceful (if impoverished) inventor could always consider an approach to the Head of Design Faculty of their nearest Art College, with a 'live' project in mind.

The companies listed in this chapter are all professionals, London-based and all specialise in product design. They have been selected primarily for their reputation and their interest in innovative design. However, the list is by no means exhaustive. It is perfectly possible to find a good design company in the regions and the **Chartered Society of Designers** will be pleased to provide a list of its members.

All the companies portrayed in this section are happy to talk to inventors; indeed, several have a personal interest in inventions themselves and have set up separate companies in-house to exploit their ideas. Any inventor thinking of using the services of one of them should talk to several before making up his mind. Each will give him a free consultation and he can be quite sure his idea will be examined in complete confidence with the utmost professional discretion. There is no need to apply for a patent in advance; indeed, it would be inadvisable to do so, as in the course of its development in-house the invention is likely to change fundamentally and possibly even eclipse its own original specification. There will be plenty of time to apply for a patent once the design is resolved.

Remember, designers are all very different in style, and the inventor may feel a closer empathy with one rather than another. Bearing in mind he is going to be working very closely with his selected designer for some time, he would do well to consider each of the companies carefully. In the final analysis he must decide what he wants for his invention. If he wants a prototype to present to a manufacturer for a licence agreement, or a fully-finished product ready to put into production through his own company, he will not find a better way of achieving his objective.

Pankhurst Design & Developments

One of the most elegant product design companies, with a crisp professional image and an impressive portfolio of products, is Pankhurst Design & Developments (PDD). Located in the heart of Fulham in south west London, it has a staff of forty designers who work in a large open plan studio with a facility for in-house model-making and rapid prototyping in adjacent, well-equipped workshops. Their expertise lies principally in small sophisticated electronic products into which they inject a high level of technical innovation. Their design concepts are entirely created in 3d CAD, using powerful workstations, and seamlessly transferred to their workshops – where CNC machines reproduce the 3d files as accurate prototypes. After product testing, these same files are sent by modem to toolmakers around the world to implement volume manufacture.

From time to time, PDD demonstrate their versatility with some classic styling solutions, perhaps for a range of international watches for Dunhill, or a revolutionary portable projection screen for Quartet in the USA. Every year for the past decade they have won at least one award for their designs.

Being such an imaginative company, it is not surprising that PDD has come up with some interesting ideas of its own. What is perhaps more unusual is that it has done something about them. Its first success was an integrated keyboard membrane moulded in silicone which interfaces electronically with the printed circuit board underneath. It is thus possible to produce a totally sealed keyboard surface, impervious to any dust or liquids that could damage the internal components of a computer. It satisfies certain demanding niche requirements such as are found in defence or medical equipment and now forms the principal product of an independent manufacturing and marketing company, Keymat Technology, with international sales and a growing order book.

In order to start the marketing company, Paul Pankhurst, founder and managing director of PDD, needed to find a source of venture capital. He came upon it almost by chance when exhibiting at Techmart at the NEC in 1987. Three years later, he inaugurated a somewhat more ambitious project with an idea born out of lateral thinking in the design studio – an integrally-moulded, all-plastic ring-binder. A preliminary enquiry revealed that there are something like ten million box files and eight million ring-binders sold each year in the UK alone. Their design origins have been lost in the mists of time. By identifying this unglamorous niche and speculatively developing an elegant product to satisfy a more demanding consumer, System

Case has set the standard for ring-binders in the 1990's. The product has since gone on sale in Canada and the USA.

Once again the problem was to secure venture capital to put the design into production, but, having produced a number of working prototypes, PDD was able to find a suitable distributor to guarantee minimum orders for the first three years and was thus able to secure the venture capital required to go into production. Launched at the beginning of 1992, the product has yet to find its niche in the UK. Interestingly, it has not affected sales of conventional ring-binders, but instead appears to have created a totally new market for 'designer' presentation folders. PDD is continuing to produce enhancements to the range.

Another example of the company's innovative approach is a portable projection screen that it presented as a concept to a client who marketed a compatible range of quality overhead and slide projectors, but had no screen of a similar standard. Once again PDD identified an unglamorous, low-profile product that had supplied the market for years and was sold almost exclusively on price. In a classic example of design initiative, PDD threw out almost every preconceived notion of projection screens and produced a design so revolutionary that, in spite of its increased cost, it has swept the market worldwide.

Paul Pankhurst has been so encouraged by the success of his forays into speculative design that he has now set up a separate in-house company called **IP Innovations**: "The objective is to encourage inventors, manufacturers and marketing companies to come to us with their ideas. If we think the notion is good enough in commercial terms, we will work with them to develop their brainchild into a product fit for the marketplace and then hopefully carry it forward into a licensing agreement, possibly with a third party for additional funding or manufacture and distribution. We would expect the inventor to carry, typically, half the cost, but for the rest we would come to an arrangement involving a share of royalties on product sales or equity participation in the case of a new company being formed."

IPI are well into their first batch products, which include a low-voltage spotlight range for a leading UK lighting manufacturer.

Wharmby Associates

Martin Wharmby was trained in product design, but has always had a keen interest in invention. Having done ten years' apprenticeship in industry as a designer, he developed the original blind spot wing mirror for motorists. The first company he showed it to ordered twenty five thousand; it took his breath away. His bank eventually paid for the tool and he managed to deliver the order just one month before the company went bankrupt. Fortunately he was paid, but his wing mirror never made it to market. Twenty-five years on, blind-spot mirrors sell in their millions.

Since then Wharmby Associates, which comprises himself and his partner Chris Garcin and two other designers, have designed numerous new products, mostly on commission for clients. However, the inventive urge is ever present and as Martin Wharmby puts it: "We would like ultimately to evolve into a company that is fuelled entirely by the commercial success of our own inventive ideas." He is already on his way to achieving his ambition.

Although the company was founded on the principles of any design consultancy and has acquired an enviable reputation for innovative and beautifully detailed designs, mainly in the area of consumer goods, the need to develop ideas of their own has always proved a powerful imperative. As a result, a separate company has been set up – **WAG Products** – that is responsible for turning simple low-tech ideas into marketable products that can be moulded, packed and sold.

Although the products it makes are essentially simple ideas, with the high degree of design and innovation that adds value, they have strong consumer appeal and sell well. One that is about to hit the market in a big way, particularly in North America, is a specially designed condom case. But their most improbable earner is a domestic electrical wall-plug extractor which sells at a rate of forty thousand units a month and earns them £12,000 a year in profits. With a wider distribution the figure could probably be quadrupled. Adds Martin Wharmby: "When we started with WAG three years ago our investment in tooling was alarming, but this year WAG Products is likely to account for over half our combined turnover."

What Wharmby Associates is learning is that doing the thing yourself is what pays. "Flogging around looking for a licence agreement is such an all-or-nothing exercise and all-too often it leads nowhere. Even if you do get an agreement, the royalties are sometimes meagre and so long in coming as to be hardly worth having in the end. Besides, you completely lose control of your product and when manufacturers are looking to cut costs they can mess almost anything up."

A perfect example of this was a beautifully designed water filter and jug that they sold to Habitat. They then took it to a reputable houseware manufacturer and offered them the idea with the order. The company bought it and put it into production but later, instead of using acrylic for the jug as specified, they used polystyrene which tainted the taste of the filtered water if left in the jug for too long. Sales have since been disappointing.

But perhaps their proudest product is the Taurus Telephone which rapidly became a classic and is selling consistently at the top end of the market, particularly in North America. It won the **D and AD Award** for British Product Design in 1991. Says Martin Wharmby: "After we had developed and sold it, the manufacturer came back and offered to buy the design from us outright. We asked for £50,000 and they offered us £5,000. In the end I'm afraid we drew the short straw."

But when it comes to dealing with inventors, Martin Wharmby keeps an open mind: "Some of them are a bit mad to say the least and we feel it our duty to discourage them from spending their money with us or anybody else for that matter. However, the stimulus of working with new ideas is very powerful for us and we are open to the approaches of practical, realistic inventors with good commercial ideas. We would probably not take a stake in their invention, but we would do all that we could to develop it into a well-designed, working product with real consumer appeal."

Lyons Ames

Few design consultancies are as receptive to the approaches of inventors than Lyons Ames. Indeed, the company, founded by Kerrin Lyons in 1985, grew out of an interest in inventions. Recalls Lyons: "I started off with a couple of ideas of my own that never quite made it, but then I was referred to a couple of entrepreneurs with a concept for a dedicated currency converter based on the principle of the pocket calculator. We designed and developed it and called it X-Changer. It went on to sell one point four million units around the world." With a royalty interest in the product, Lyons Ames was set firmly on its feet.

Located above a telescope shop in Farringdon Road, London, Lyons Ames operates out of comfortable, well-appointed offices with studio and workshop facilities. On display are the various products it has been associated with; it is a surprising mix. On the one hand is a range of beautifully designed video cameras and accessory cases carrying the Sony label which display an aesthetic worthy of a fashion designer. Elsewhere are small consumer electrical products which have become classics of their type; the compact pocket translator being an elegant example.

Having an ongoing relationship with a client like Sony is a gratifying, reassuring position for any design company, but Lyons likes the challenge that inventors and independent entrepreneurs present to him: "It gives us the opportunity to be associated with the sort of innovative new ideas that larger companies seldom get involved in."

Although they rarely accept royalties in lieu of fees, Lyons Ames will do all it can to help the inventor maximise his resources. But as the project progresses, the creative and technical input from the designer often enhances and surpasses the original brief from the client. Indeed, advice and assistance invariably stray outside the confines of the design brief and embrace a broad commercial strategy for the product as a whole. This may involve identifying additional applications and other commercial concepts for the core idea.

One of the most intriguing products Lyons Ames are ever likely to design was undertaken for a Monaco-based entrepreneur who came to them with a novel idea, but an almost impossible brief: to design a one-handed condom applicator, to enhance sexual spontaneity! Fortunately, once the right technical solution had occurred to their design team, Lyons Ames took the brief seriously, consulting sex experts, condom specialists and consumer researchers during the remarkably brief gestation period of the product itself. A new production line was rapidly set up in France, and the product is now selling well across Europe. Awarding Lyons Ames 'Packaging Innovation of the Year' (with perhaps just a touch of irony), the Design Award judges added a special mention of the importance of developments in this 'sensitive' area.

With an eye on the future, Lyons Ames has taken the unusual step of setting up a separate production company, KLIP, for the purposes of developing, manufacturing and marketing their own ideas along with those of other inventors. Explains Lyons: "The idea is to brainstorm new concepts, obtain patent cover and then turn them into marketable products with the facility to sell them ourselves. If we can make it work for us, then hopefully we can offer the whole package to the inventor, to get new products quickly into the marketplace."

Sams Design

Working out of a high street studio in north London, a short distance from the North Circular Road, Bernard Sams has been designing small, innovative mechanical products (mostly in plastic) for over twenty five years. His experience has made him a master of his art. The numerous design awards that he has won bear testimony to this. His designs have a reputation for incorporating definitive solutions which spawn generations of similar products. For instance, the modern supermarket labeller (now twenty years old), the self-inking rubber stamp and the dial-a-dose Novopen insulin injection regulator for diabetics have all set the standard in their field.

With his small staff of five, all of whom are highly inventive, Sams likes a fairly open 'find the solution' kind of brief from his clients. The insulin dose injector was a case in point. A team of Danish engineers, in co-operation with an international design group, had been working on the problem for two years without success. Finally, facing defeat, they turned to Sams Design who solved the problem in three weeks.

Naturally, Sams has a stack of patents to his name, but generally he assigns them to his clients in exchange for royalties. In fact, he has been known to send a company packing when it refused to grant him a royalty, which only goes to show how short-sighted some companies can be, given the longevity of his designs. But he is somewhat ambivalent about the reality of royalties: "If you work for royalties alone the risks are too great, which goes for speculative design as well. It is very tempting to spend studio time working on your pet idea – and we have done so in the past – but I have my staff to pay and when a project can take several years to mature, it is a big gamble."

Bernard Sams is very open to approaches from innovators who have practical ideas involving the sort of problems he likes to tackle. And he is only too happy to have inventors referred to him by institutions such as the Design Council or the British Technology Group. In fact, one such is Atmosol which featured in the finals of the Prince of Wales Award in 1990. Invented by Bill Warren and promoted by his partner, Gerry Taylor, it is likely to set the standard for inert gas and air-pressurised aerosol systems in the next decade. Adds Sams: 'If we like an idea enough we might offer the inventor the opportunity to continue sharing costs with us in exchange for a royalty agreement when the product comes to market.'

Product First

Barley Mow Passage in Chiswick is a huge old wallpaper warehouse converted into a labyrinth of offices and studios and rented out to a broad spectrum of creative companies. On the first floor in a large, well laid-out studio is Product First. Although engaged in a variety of design activities, it is, as its name implies, first and foremost a new product development company.

The consultancy has a reputation for strong innovative input into its design solutions and has developed a revolutionary range of audio headphones, for instance, for Ross Electronics, which resulted from a very thorough examination of the market and its requirements. John Boult, the consultancy's Managing Director, explains his company's philosophy thus: "Product FIRST aims to get our clients' products *first* into the market, and then to keep them in *first* position by being creative, using the latest IT technology and by thoroughly planning the design process. Working for some of the world's most innovative companies such as Unilever, 3M and Siemens means that we do not really have the time to engage in any speculative design work of our own."

However, Product First is keen to work with inventors, believing that good design input at the early stages of a project will increase the likelihood of investor funding. Recent work for inventors has resulted in some interesting products, says Boult, such as a wasp trap, a folding lavatory seat for children, an in-car desk and a device for detecting hidden obstacles, such as pipes and pillars, behind walls. 'Tracker' is now featured in many design catalogues and has become something of a consumer classic as well as a commercial success.

Boult, who was formerly a member of the selection panel for the Design Council's Innovation Service, is unequivocal about his company's interest in innovative design: "Often clients are unclear about what they really want and look to us to take the initiative in making suggestions. We try to be a catalyst within the companies we work for and indeed act as our own product champions in nurturing our designs forward into production. We endeavour to cultivate a vital and integrated relationship with all our clients which we have found in the long run is often very rewarding."

Industrial Design Consultancy

Industrial Design Consultancy (IDC) is a large and well-established practice located at Datchet, a short distance outside London along the M4 corridor. Unlike many design consultancies of its size that have tended to embrace a broad spectrum of design disciplines, IDC focuses its primary skills on product development, which is where its strength lies: developing products that are cost-effective to manufacture, styling that appeals to the public, making them want to buy, and that makes the client money. Indeed, its abilities in this area are impressive. Its well-equipped workshops include state-of-the-art vacuum casting in PU resin, Pro-Engineer, Pro-Design, Varimetrix 3D CAD and CNC machining. As a result, IDC can see sophisticated projects right through from concept to fully working prototype ready for production.

Having established a large client base, most of IDC's work is briefled on a fee-paying basis, but the consultancy is happy to consider royalties on occasion.

One of the consultancy's initiatives is regularly to take a stand at **Domotechnica**, the huge annual domestic appliance and housewares exhibition at Cologne in Germany. This has enabled the consultancy to make some valuable contacts and take on work that has put it on the map as a European design agency. Comments John Stimpson, IDC's marketing manager: "People in this profession are increasingly looking towards Japan for jobs, but in my view there is more than enough work here on our own doorstep if we only go out and look for it. It is just a question of establishing contacts and enhancing our reputation."

For the inventor who has a complex design to resolve, IDC has an enormous depth of experience in electro-mechanical disciplines. With its contacts in British industry, it is in a strong position to help inventors sell their ideas as well as develop them. Acting as product champions, IDC can bring new ideas to the attention of existing customers, with many of whom it has long-standing relationships. Adds Stimpson: "We are a very British company and with the huge reservoir of creative talent that exists in this country we are only too pleased if we can act as a catalyst in our capacity as designers to channel some of this ingenuity into British industry. It ean only go to strengthen our own position and the long term industrial ability of this country."

The Innovations Group

Mail order is one of the best ways for a manufacturer to assess the market potential of a new product. It has several advantages. Apart from promoting the product directly to a large audience, and having the space to illustrate and explain the product fully, it offers a unique opportunity to develop a direct relationship with the consumer, an opportunity which is denied to new merchandise in the normal retail environment. It provides a means of obtaining feedback – you can easily find out where any problems may lie – and it enables you to test different designs, packaging and price points. It also cuts out the middle man. However, mail order marketing can be tricky to get right, and it pays to accept professional help. Most direct marketing agencies understand their business all right, but they may not understand yours... and few are prepared to share the risk of launching a new product. However, there is one specialist who understands the business of invention extremely well...

Everyone who reads the Sunday papers has come across the *Innovations* catalogue. As the original mail order compendium of innovative consumer products, distributed as a loose insert in the weekend press, it has spawned a host of imitators; not least of its occasionally tongue-in-cheek copywriting style – but still remains by far the most distinctive and successful publication in its field. The reason is simple: the catalogue seems to have a hotline to all the newest and brightest product ideas. What you discover in *Innovations* today you will find in your High Street tomorrow.

Innovations was launched in 1985 and has since become one of the main catalogue brands of the Innovations group of companies, now part of The Burton Group Plc. The group is dedicated to sourcing and marketing innovative consumer products all over the world. With a mailing list of over three million in the UK alone and foreign distributors in major markets worldwide, no other organisation offers the inventor a better opportunity of introducing his idea to the consumer. In fact, it can often provide the innovator with a commercial shop window when no other avenue exists.

The group receives about a hundred submissions a week from individuals and companies that would like their products to be included in one of their next series of quarterly catalogues. They also source internationally, and introduce over two thousand new products each year to the British public. Many of them fail to reach their anticipated sales and are soon dropped, but others do well and earn their place in subsequent publications.

But of all the initiatives at *Innovations*, the most far-reaching was the setting up of the Product Development Unit In the past,

Innovations would sometimes be presented with a wonderful idea from an inventor which neither he nor they could do anything about, both sides effectively lacking the necessary means for development. Finally it was decided to put together an in-house team of electrical engineers to develop these ideas into commercial products. At least one soon turned out to be a world-beater: the Innovations Battery Charger can trickle-charge any standard domestic battery back to full power up to ten times before it has to be discarded. Billions of batteries which hitherto ended up prematurely in the bin can now effectively be recycled.

Clive Beharrell, one of the founding directors of the company, is an authentic champion of new products. "I have always enjoyed discovering new ideas," he says, "and it is our intention to continue to seek new and better ways of allowing the British inventor to bring his brainchild to market."

The opportunity offered to inventors through *Innovations* is enormous. They are able to provide a series of flexible packages which can be tailor-made to suit each situation and individual. Most requirements can be met, from an inventor wishing to assign his patent rights to the company in exchange for a one-off lump sum, to a whole range of licensing agreements involving development collaboration with the inventor linked to investment backing by the company. All are secured by a percentage royalty payment in the event of sales. The opportunity for the independent inventor to present his product to the end-user in a uniquely persuasive fashion is offered only by The Innovations Group.

Clive Beharrell is optimistic about the prospects for his company: "We are a large and very creative organisation with a worldwide distribution network. We are looking for products with international appeal which we can distribute through our wholesale arm, Innovations International. Direct response mail order offers unique exposure for novel products, creating an awareness and demand for them far beyond their initial sales. It is in effect a potent form of advertising. Our catalogues sit around people's homes for a long time. We believe direct response marketing is a trend that is set to grow. *Innovations* has evolved from the 'eighties into a trading group with a clear vision for the 'nineties and beyond. As a company we like to realise our visions".

4

Invention Competitions

The British have long been recognised as an inventive race. Some surveys suggest that over half of the best inventions of this century have come from the Anglo-Saxon imagination, although we have recently been overtaken in the innovation stakes by the USA and Japan. It is hardly surprising then that so many national invention competitions are held in the United Kingdom – the problem being, to know which competitions are being run, when, and where to find information about them. Industry is a notoriously fickle sponsor and several major companies like BP, NatWest and Toshiba who have allied their brand names with innovation in the past, incidentally creating high-profile opportunities for thousands of British inventors to showcase their ideas, are no longer in the business of promoting inventions.

But if you can find one to enter, such as the John Logie Baird awards (you'll need to declare Scottish ancestry), there is nothing like winning a prestigious national competition to revitalise your invention. Notwithstanding the media coverage that corporate sponsors derive from these high-profile championships, the benefits bestowed on the winner enhances immeasurably, the credibility of their invention. In some cases it will have been been selected from thousands of entries and has been examined and sanctioned by the pre-eminent people in their field. It is an accolade to be proud of.

The crucial thing is to capitalise quickly on the elevated status and public awareness of your new invention. The moment of glory will soon pass. Whatever your objectives, you must strike while the iron is hot. Perhaps licensing is your preferred route. Put together a portfolio of publicity to send out to suitable companies. Offer it to invention brokers and allow them the opportunity to present it to industry on your behalf. Go to your bank manager and convince him your invention now justifies his financial collaboration. Seek out venture capitalists through suitable sources. Get people on board who can help you and push it for all it is worth while you may.

One of the most satisfying aspects of invention competitions is that they cost you next to nothing to enter, so you have nothing to lose. However, you stand little chance of winning unless your invention has got what it takes, and what it takes can vary from one competition to another. Always try and give yourself an edge. Judges are impressed by professionalism.

Make sure you comply correctly with the rules. Present your invention in the best possible manner. If, for instance, you are allowed to submit photographs, make sure that they at least look professionally taken. Models are sometimes accepted as entry material; make sure they look the part and work well. Consult a designer if need be. But above all, do not enter your invention prematurely. Wait until you have a pre-production prototype you can submit that is indistinguishable from the real thing. This will certainly influence the judges and indicate its commercial potential. Try and stand out from the crowd and give your entry every opportunity of making a good impression.

Being in the form of a competition, the DTI's SMART scheme is included in this section, although its objectives are rather different from the rest. Like the Prince of Wales Award, it comes in two parts, each of which can be won consecutively by the same company. It is normally aimed at small companies with an innovative idea for a new product which they want to develop and put into production. The sums of money awarded may be substantial, but the winners are required to match it in part with their own funds. It is very hard for an individual to win an award unless he has a small production company through which he can develop his idea.

The Prince of Wales Award for Innovation

The Prince of Wales Award for Innovation was the first, and remains the most prestigious, national invention competition. Inspired and inaugurated by Prince Charles in the early 1980s, it is now firmly established as a major annual event and screened as a special pro-gramme on BBC TV's *Tomorrow's World*. The finalists and overall winner receive extensive publicity which goes a long way towards helping their inventions become significant commercial successes.

The organisation responsible for running the competition, from sifting through the initial entries to selecting the final winners, is **Business in the Community**. The process starts for BIC in early September when it sends out a large mailshot to every organisation and institution across the country that might have some contact with inventors. It also includes inventors on its own database and any indi-viduals from whom it has received inquiries. The competition is open to absolutely anyone. The closing date for entry is the end of January the following year.

The comprehensive application form requires entrants to answer questions about their inventions in some detail, particularly with regard to commercial potential. Inventions of any kind can be entered, the only stipulation being that they should not have been in commer-cial production for more than one year. The entrant is encouraged to send any supporting material considered relevant, such as illustrations or photographs, video recordings and even models and prototypes. If the invention is in production, the product itself can be submitted. The competition regularly receives several hundred entries.

As soon as entry for the competition closes, the selection process commences to separate the wheat from the chaff. The preliminary judging panel comprises fifteen members elected from a wide range of professional disciplines. They retire to a comfortable country hotel for a long weekend, charged initially with reducing the submissions to a manageable number. This takes about two days and leaves the panel with around fifteen per cent of the entries to look at in more detail; the object is to narrow the number down to a final twenty one. Some heated discussions inevitably take place, but the final selection is invariably unanimous – a shortlist of technically-sound commercial ideas.

The next stage takes place in March. A final judging panel is formed, comprising ten highly qualified experts in various fields, including the commercial arena. Their job is to select six out of the final twenty one to go forward to the Innovation Stage. Stage two, the Production Stage, effectively lasts two years. During this time the inventor or the business that has developed the invention, is encouraged to maximise the commercial potential of the product. It is the degree of commercial progress achieved during this period and the prospects for future market growth that, as much as anything, determine the final winner.

Around the same time as the first wave of new entries are being assessed, the finalists from two years previously are being visited by members of the final judging panel to examine their development. In some cases it can be very disappointing, but in others the commercial nettle has been grasped and significant marketing progress has been made.

The final programme in the current series of *Tomorrow's World* is given over to highlighting the six finalists and their progress. At the end of the programme the overall winner is presented with the trophy by Prince Charles. Invariably the winner is a technical and commercial world beater and graphically illustrates the inventive talent for which Britain is so highly regarded.

John Logie Baird Awards

As a part of its ongoing effort to promote innovation in Scotland, **Scottish Innovation** runs a national competition called the John Logie Baird Awards. Its honorary president is the widow of John Logie Baird – who, as the originator of television in the 1920s, is one of Scotland's most famous sons. It started in a small way in 1988 and

130

was confined to the Strathclyde region around Glasgow. But such was its success that it has now expanded to cover the whole of Scotland The competition embraces every aspect of innovation, with regional competitions covering the areas of the Local Enterprise Companies, and the National competition which covers the whole of Scotland. Winners and other 'Highly Commended' projects from the regional competitions are put forward to the National competition, which has three categories:

* Most innovative project by a company
* Most innovative project by an individual
* Best new innovative idea

The project manager for the whole scheme is Brian Wilson, who over-sees the competition and processes the applications. Indeed, in the early days he and his colleagues tried to visit every entrant personally, but as the competition has grown, so this has become impractical. Nevertheless, he is responsible for making the initial selections to be put before an independent panel of judges.

The competition opens in January and closes around the end of August each year, with the overall winners being announced at an award ceremony during October. From a total entry of two hundred and fifty, a short-list of twenty four will be selected, and from this the judges select three finalists in each category. In the past every finalist has received £1,000 with a further £5,000 going to the overall winner in each section. The money may be useful, but the attendant publicity is perhaps even more so, giving a winner the credibility to approach more substantial sources of capital. In the case of a company, it can provide a timely fillip to their fortunes and, for an individual the encouragement to develop his or her brainchild into a commercial product.

DTI SMART awards

Of all the government grants and initiatives available to the private inventor or small firm through the DTI, SMART has been one of the most prestigious and valuable. Almost any technology with the potential to be transformed into a commercial product has a real chance of winning an award. Presented in the form of a competition, its purpose is to provide funds for a technical and commercial feasibility study, and then to take the project on to development stage. The sums of money can be very substantial.

The inspiration for SMART came from an American initiative to encourage small firms to win government contracts. But in effect the UK version bears little resemblance to its role model. It was inaugurated in 1986 as a pilot scheme with a mere twenty awards. But since then it has been formalised into a national competition which announces one hundred and eighty award winners every year, costing the government some £8 million in grant money. In 1995, additional awards were made as a consequence of some areas qualifying for European Regional Development funds.

The competition usually opens at the beginning of the year and closes by the end of April. It is open to individuals and small firms employing up to fifty people. It is predominantly aimed at developing technology. The selection process is pegged to a points system based on meeting certain criteria. The degree of innovation in an idea is given top priority. Thereafter, the calibre of the team associated with it, together with its technical merits and its prospects of being turned into a commercial success are taken into account – along with the applicant's actual financial requirement. The whole proposal is examined very carefully by technical experts, financial advisers and commercial assessors to ascertain whether the project meets the exacting requirements of the competition. It is also established whether a winner would be in a position to meet his share of the investment.

The competition is administered by the DTI Directorates of government offices throughout the UK; the Scottish Office, the Welsh Office and the Northern Ireland Department of Economic Development. In order to spread the awards evenly throughout the country, each region is allocated a specific number at the outset. This can vary from year to year, depending on past performance. It makes for a degree of healthy rivalry between the regions. However, a number of additional awards are held in reserve and are apportioned on merit to the regions by the national co-ordinators of the scheme.

Applicants for an award are required to submit a comprehensive entry outlining the details of their proposal. In 1995, over eleven hundred applications were received. These are subjected to the scoring system described earlier. The most promising ideas are initially selected in a screening exercise carried out by the regions in close consultation with approved advisers. The applicants who survive this stage are normally visited and their proposals looked at in more detail.

The award cannot be granted retrospectively. In other words, it is properly presumed that the innovator cannot proceed without the money. The maximum grant available under the old SMART was £45,000, representing three-quarters of the total eligible project costs on a £60,000 award. The innovator is required to make up the balance.

Once awarded, a project will be monitored carefully to see that targets are being met and the money spent as designated. However, one of the attractions of SMART is that the first cheque, amounting to one third of the total, is presented in hand at the outset, often at a formal award ceremony with all the attendant publicity, which can get a winner off to a flying start. Thereafter, payments are made against approved expenditure.

Projects that have met their initial targets but clearly need further funding in order to proceed, can apply for a second tranche of capital but, as before, any grant must be matched in equal part by the originator's own money. This of course can come from any source – banks, venture capitalists, private investors – but it is likely to be substantial. The maximum combined grant has been pegged at 200,000 ECU, approximately £250,000 (1997). However, changes are anticipated in the SMART scheme as a consequence of the 1997 election. Further information can be obtained from the DTI.

5

Invention Brokers

No group of individuals is more committed to helping inventors than invention brokers. It is how they make their living. Broadly, they fall into two categories – the general invention broker and the specialist. Of the two, the latter tends to be the most effective. He brings to bear an abundance of experience and above all a wealth of personal connections within his chosen field. If an invention broker believes in your idea, and does not charge you a fortune for promoting it, you have a strong chance of seeing your idea appear on the market.

When choosing an agent to act on your behalf, it is a matter of 'horses for courses'.... Try at least to establish if those under consideration are accustomed to handling your sort of invention. Press them on whether they have previously had any success with a similar idea. Find out how they operate and how active they will be in targeting your product to appropriate companies.

The best invention brokers do not charge you directly for marketing your idea, but take a stake in its subsequent success. In doing so they are nailing their colours firmly to your mast. If they fail to sell your invention they will lose their investment in terms of the time and money they have taken to promote it. Since they have a clear vested interest in its success, you will have little to lose and much to gain should they succeed.

Each broker has evolved independently and operates to a separate set of criteria. Taken as a group they represent a broad spectrum of possibilities for the inventor. Specialist invention brokers can only be used if your product comes into their category. But the general brokers will take on anything they feel they can place. In the majority of cases their up-front fees are very modest and well worth your investment.

When they require you to make a further personal investment to improve the product, it is probably in your interests to do so. The better the product, the better their chance of selling it. You need have no worries about relying on the discretion of professional brokers. As with product designers, they are bound by professional ethics not to allow anything to slip inadvertently into the public domain. You have nothing to fear if your product as yet has no patent; they will tell you in advance if they think you need one.

One note of caution should be added here: all the brokers listed in this section are bone fide, but there are some out there that are not. I would advise any inventor considering using the services of a broker to avoid, as a general rule, anyone who advertises for inventor's ideas in the business-to-business pages of the national press.

Product International Ltd

Strategically, the village of Stone in Staffordshire would seem an unlikely location for what is one of the best-known invention brokers in the country. Product International Ltd. satisfies certain important requirements for any organisation that sets out actively to market inventions for inventors; it cannot make a living unless it achieves results.

Product International Ltd. grew out of a much older organisation founded in the 1970s which functioned as a 'hands-on' advisory service to manufacturers. The primary activity is still the same, that of assisting companies to grow through the introduction of new products, although the broader management skills within the company enable it to provide a wide range of advisory services to its client companies. It is very much a market-led company and, because it is essentially working for industrial clients has the opportunity to take onto its product database new products from a wide variety of sources, for example Local Enterprise Agencies, Chambers of Commerce and Business Links. More importantly, it has built up a reputation which ensures a steady stream of new inventions for evaluation from all over the UK and overseas.

All inventions accepted by the company undergo rigorous appraisal for commercial viability and every idea taken aboard is targeted carefully towards the appropriate manufacturing sector. The executive team are experienced industrialists who have spent a considerable time working in manufacturing and marketing. No more than four new products are taken on in any one week, although for some that are turned down initially, additional information and even further development work may be requested.

Once past the appraisal, the inventor will be informed in writing if his product has been successful. There is a one-off fee at this stage of £250 to cover costs, but the inventor at least knows that his idea has been specifically targeted to potential manufacturers, and its commercial viability assessed in the marketplace. Clients are asked to sign a confidentiality undertaking before the idea is shown to them.

On achieving a successful introduction, Product International Ltd. undertake to negotiate for the very best terms, although the final decision is left to the inventor. The consultancy takes a standard fee of ten per cent of the overall financial package, which otherwise consists of expenses fees and royalties to the inventor. But they do not make any money unless they actually succeed in introducing your idea to a manufacturer. Consequently, they point out, the inventor has nothing to lose – and everything to gain – by going to them.

Once the product is placed, Product International Ltd. continues to monitor its commercial progress. Over the years, it has built up a network of connections worldwide, creating potential for further commercial development opportunities

Pax Technology Transfer Ltd.

John Emanuel speaks four European languages fluently. He needs every one of them. His job is marketing new ideas all over the world. Since setting up Pax Technology Transfer in 1978, he has been involved with numerous successful inventions and has cultivated an impressive network of international associates. If he thinks your idea is worth his investment, he could become a formidable ally in bringing your idea to market.

Although committed to serious business prospects, he admits to having a soft spot for inventors and will consider even the most ambitious of schemes. However, commercial reality remains paramount so, above all, he will be looking for evidence of the value of the invention. Most inventors are referred to his company by first-call advisers such as patent agents, innovation counsellors and technology managers. These will have acted as a filtering mechanism, passing on only their most promising clients. But he still likes to get a feel for an idea before agreeing to see it and expects his first contact to be by phone. He is ready to talk to anyone with a new idea for ten to fifteen minutes without charge.

If his interest is aroused, he may propose a meeting with the inventor. This constitutes a presentation either to himself or one of his colleagues on the basis of a one hour meeting, at a fixed fee. Its purpose is to evaluate the product more fully and is designed to benefit both parties. It is an evaluation and strategy session for the invention determined by its potential validity. But no matter how ingenious it may be, unless it meets certain commercial criteria, it will only be of academic interest to Pax. However, the inventor can expect his money's worth and will get some sound advice on advancing his invention . This situation occurs around once or twice a month.

Every so often Pax meets an idea that it likes enough to invite on board. It will then propose a working agreement with the inventor in exchange for a portion of his equity. This is unlikely to amount to much, being typically only around twenty per cent. In fact, if Pax feels its risk requires much more than thirty per cent, it will probably reject it. A nominal agreement fee is also attached. Once signed up, the inventor can expect some action. Pax is in the business of making money and will bring all its considerable expertise to bear on marketing the idea.

What sets Pax Technology apart from other general invention brokers is its international perspective. No other UK invention broker is so well connected overseas. It vastly increases the market opportunities for a new product. Japan and the United States are as important territories to Pax as Continental Europe.

In addition to knowing many thousands of companies, Pax is also retained by quite a number to look for new products. This gives it immediate access to a corporate world invariably closed to the independent inventor and many of Pax's best deals are done this way. At all times the commercial objective remains clearly in focus and helps to keep the programme on course.

Another very valuable service offered by Pax to inventors and small companies alike is what it calls 'project broking'. This is usually for a fixed hourly fee, but can be in exchange for equity. In general, it entails every aspect of bringing a product to market and a programme can be set out to suit the client. In most cases, this will involve finding ways to finance, develop and market a new idea. It may include seeking private or venture capital, finding suitable technical or business partners, offering advice on drawing up a business plan, formulating market research, structuring a marketing agenda, creating a whole programme to meet an objective and generally helping a client to get his act together and present his case in a credible fashion.

In addition, one of Pax's greatest strengths is in negotiating licence agreements, in which it is hugely experienced. Targeting a potential licensee, negotiating a contract and closing the deal is perhaps the most daunting endeavour any inventor ever has to undertake on his own, and professional assistance from Pax can make all the difference to achieving a result.

John Emanuel sums up the service his company has to offer: "In consultancy terms, we are really facilitators. We can help an inventor to translate his brainchild into a business proposition with prudence, discretion and, above all, knowledge, and then we can take his idea to the market place and sell it for him"' It is a package that most brokerage companies would find hard to match.

Inventorlink Ltd

Located in central London, Inventorlink, founded by Richard Paine and Charles Dawes in the early 1980s, is one of the UK's premier international invention brokers. It certainly has a high profile, having received over the years extensive editorial coverage in the national and international press. Its role is to provide a direct marketing link between individual inventors and their ideas and manufacturing industry, both in the UK and overseas. Its reputation rests on some notable successes.

Although it doesn't advertise, Inventorlink is sufficiently well known to be approached by many individuals with their inventions. Patent agents also sometimes point people in their direction. Another important source of ideas is the Patent Office. Of the several hundred new patents published in the UK each week, perhaps twenty might be individual applications and these are screened for good ideas. If Inventorlink thinks that they have some commercial potential, it writes to the inventor offering its services. A selection panel sits once a week, and sifts through all the ideas that have been gathered in during the previous seven days. Of the twenty or so normally considered, only three or four are selected for further consideration; the rest will be told by letter that Inventorlink is unable to help them market their idea.

At this point the inventor whose idea has proved of some interest is invited to attend Inventorlink's offices or send complete information of the invention by post for it to be fully assessed. The inventor is also sent a folder containing a confidentiality agreement which he is asked to sign and a product marketing programme which lists the various stages through which it is hoped the invention will progress towards a signed licence agreement with a suitable manufacturing company.

Charles Dawes is responsible for reviewing each invention in detail with its originator. He normally spends about an hour talking to the inventor about the idea and getting a clear picture of its development and commercial possibilities. The consultation is entirely free and without obligation. If both sides are then happy to proceed, the inventor is invited to make a single contribution towards the cost of promoting the product, which is offered in three clear options. The first is a £3,250 payment pegged to a seven and a half per cent share of all income received as a result of a successful licence agreement being achieved. The second is for £2,500 and a fifteen per cent stake; and the third £1,700 with a thirty five per cent stake. Amounts are subject to VAT where applicable.

Richard Paine stresses that regardless of which option the inventor takes, the service remains exactly the same. Although these sums may appear somewhat high, Paine maintains they fall well below the substantial amount it can cost to promote any new product effectively. Around half take up the offer, which means Inventorlink handles around one hundred inventions a year for its clients.

The marketing programme is spearheaded by *Inventions International*, a twice-monthly publication which describes and illustrates up to ten new ideas in each issue. It is circulated to industrial subscribers who pay a modest fee for the privilege of a preview of the journal. However, a wider net is cast using Inventorlink's extensive database to identify those known to be looking for new ideas. Explains Paine: "One never knows when a seed is going to fall on fertile ground. So often I am surprised by who takes up an idea." The invention is also added to the company's database or new product register, which is shown to companies that visit Inventorlink in search of new products.

Once a company has shown interest in a concept, it is asked to sign a confidentiality agreement before being shown the invention. A continuous process is then set in motion which may extend into years rather than months of laborious consultation, aimed at eventually signing a licence agreement with the interested company. Adds Paine: "!t is a protracted and complicated process and our credibility and tenacity are all important. We are on first-name terms with many chief and senior executives of major companies, which helps us to get a foot in the door – but at the end of the day no company is going to take up and develop a new idea unless it thinks it is going to make money out of it."

Oxford HealthCare Ltd

Michael Ely is a happy man. He has good reason to be; he makes his living doing a job he loves and in all probability he is unique in his speciality; he sells medical inventions to industry.

It was not how he started out. For many years he literally did the reverse; he sold devices from manufacturers to the medical profession. It was at a time, in the early 1970s, when disposables like syringes and face masks were becoming mandatory and opportunities to get into this lucrative market were proliferating. For an energetic young sales-man there were boundless possibilities. The more he worked in the field, the more he saw niche needs for new ideas.

Occasionally companies would ask him to look out for new prod-ucts to add to their ranges. Small companies would start up making a particular device, and Ely would bring it to the attention of his client company. It was a fringe activity that gradually came more and more into focus. He was also cultivating a lot of useful contacts within the industry.

As with any other industry, inventors were increasingly pestering the major manufacturers with their ideas. Formal departments were set up to deal with them. As usual, it was really nothing more than a smoke-screen. Companies had their own R&D departments and were wary of ideas coming in from outside, although they had to be seen to be dealing with inventors in a considerate and acceptable manner and not merely dismissing them out of hand. Nevertheless, they did need new products and a means of sourcing them was essential. Ely knew the profession inside-out and what it wanted in the way of practical product improvements. It was a situation he was well placed to exploit.

In 1989 he left his comfortable job and set up on his own as a con-sultant. Although marketing inventions clearly interested him, at first he did not see it as his main activity. His knowledge of the market was such that he was able to advise companies which product areas pre-sented the best prospects for future growth. But in his first week he met a man who had developed a protective sheath for disposable syringes who asked him to market it for him. Ely knew all the right people to take it to. Shortly afterwards, an entrepreneur who was also a brilliant engineer came to him with a syringe that would work only once before failing. It was exactly what the industry wanted. He licensed it to a manufacturer in Germany on a five per cent gross sales royalty. It is likely to make its inventor a lot of money.

In the years since he set up Oxford Healthcare, Ely has become a specialist broker of medical inventions. He sees his role very clearly: "The problem with many inventors is that they muddy the waters prematurely with the wrong approaches to the best companies. What companies want are products that work well, fulfil a recognised need and can be made at a reasonable price. They also want someone they know who talks their own language. I am in a position to offer them exactly what they want."

Although fiercely competitive, the medical industry, even internationally, is a closed club with a limited number of major players. The lone inventor is a rank outsider, but with the help of Michael Ely he may just find the key to the door.

Seven Towns

When it comes to specialist invention broking few can claim to have more experience than Tom Kremer of Seven Towns. In 1969 he went into partnership with a colleague to invent and market new toys and games, but they soon found that their creative output exceeded their capacity to manufacture. Licensing became the obvious route and the selling of ideas quickly replaced the selling of products. Word began to get out that they were able to place ideas with toy companies and a trickle of originators began to use their services. It was thus by chance that Seven Towns became what was probably the first invention broker in this country.

Nowadays the company is geared to creativity and the sourcing, selection and development of novel games and toys. Most ideas are generated in-house and developed in their own well-equipped workshops, but they also extensively use the specialist services of outside designers and model makers. The company is happy to have a steady stream of ideas coming in from outside which it evaluates for originality and viability. Most come from first-timers, but there is a handful of professional inventors who use its services as well. Kremer stresses the value of such external input: "The toy industry is an evolutionary animal that responds quickly to new fads and fashions; it knows where it is going and in the main knows how to get there. But the really big revolutionary new ideas often come from outside. We never know when one is going to walk in through our door."

One of the biggest ever for Seven Towns was the Rubik's Cube which literally sold hundreds of millions of puzzles all over the world. Unfortunately, by the time Kremer discovered it, it was already in the public domain and he was unable to prevent much of the plagiarism that surrounded it. Seven Towns eventually managed to control the sale of seventy five million units, which went a long way towards enhancing their credibility. They now handle all of Professor Rubik's multifarious inventions.

The procedure adopted by Seven Towns in assessing outside ideas is not dissimilar to that of most invention brokers. Inventors are encouraged to submit their concepts for initial appraisal. If this generates a spark of interest, they are asked to come in and discuss their idea in more detail. Such meetings determine whether there is anything worth pursuing. If so, the inventor is invited to sign a development agreement with the company. No money changes hands, but the terms are that if Seven Towns eventually licenses the final product, development costs such as model making will be deducted from earned income. It would seem a good arrangement for an originator.

Part of the reason is that Seven Towns does not foster an idea in the role of an agent, but adopts it entirely by taking it fully into its own development programme. Accordingly, as part of its contract with the inventor, it requires complete freedom to develop it in the way it wants. Some inventors find this hard to accept; so, in order to avoid any misunderstandings at a later stage, the terms of the agreement are settled from the outset. This way, no matter what eventually emerges, the inventor's percentage is secure.

But the whole development process can take a very long time and the marketing phase sometimes even longer, so many variables are involved. According to Kremer, Seven Towns recently sold a product that had been in its portfolio for over ten years. Selling a new idea is never easy and, in spite of all the company's investment and knowledge of the industry, it expects to place no more than a quarter to a third of its portfolio. The rest reverts back to their originators.

Seven Towns, which operates offices in New York and Tokyo as well as London, is a hugely profitable company. Its royalty stream obviously fluctuates significantly, but over the last ten years it has never fallen below $2 million in any one year. Of this, about two-thirds is generated from its own ideas and one-third from independents. Of course, much of this money comes from well-established products that are still earning an excellent income. Kremer offers his definition of a good toy: "That which gives the maximum of magic with the minimum of cost; something with a high 'aah!' factor; that element of surprise which can enchant both adult and child alike. Really great toys can create magic out of nothing." But he adds a word of caution: "It is so hard to create something really original. I take on about two per cent of all I see and, even after extensive development, I still sell less than half of what I have. Inventors find it hard to understand that so much has been done before. But if you have an idea that you think might have something, go first to the guy who knows the field before you go anywhere else; if he takes an interest in it you are probably already half way there."

Games Talk

Over the years, Iain Kidney of Games Talk, the specialist invention broker par excellence, has seen the board games industry from every possible point of view. In his understanding and knowledge of the market he is without peer. If Kidney tells you your game is going nowhere, you would do well to believe him.

At the age of twenty four, Kidney was put in charge of the games and toys buying division of W.H. Smith with a £25 million purchasing budget. He rose rapidly to the responsibility. Within a short time he was acting as a consultant to major games manufacturers that wanted to improve the products they were offering to the market leader. But like most games buyers, he was increasingly pestered by the independents. Many of his counterparts dismissed them altogether, but being somewhat more sympathetic, he soon realised their problems. For a start, they displayed all the symptoms of the lone inventor – imagination, initiative, enthusiasm and a total misunderstanding of the marketplace. For what they did not know was what the public would actually buy. Kidney also came to realise just how many people invent board games.

His course was clear. In 1989 he left a promising career at W.H. Smith and set up Games Talk with a colleague. He was not short of contracts, having already made his reputation among the majors. He was soon inundated with consultancy work – games appraisal, product development, play testing, sourcing, designing, naming; he was asked to do it all, but after a while the pattern began to change. The bountiful flow of submissions from independent inventors to the toy companies was becoming increasingly irksome to them and they started to pass on these ideas piecemeal to Games Talk. Kidney was willing and able to look at them all.

The quantity of ideas he receives is formidable: more than *six thousand* submissions annually, enough to overwhelm a lesser professional. But as Kidney says of himself: "I can often judge the commercial potential of a game within sixty seconds of looking at it; originality is the key to everything. People still think they can devise a game based on the Monopoly™ principle; they are thirty years out of date. The reason that Monopoly™ still sells so well is that it is so well-known, but a newer – even possibly better – game along the same lines has got no chance; the market has become far too sophisticated. It is hard for the average inventor to understand this. As a general rule, I would advise people to avoid inventing strategy games of any sort and theme games are just as bad. No matter how good they are in themselves, there is no way I can sell them." This statement explains why Games Talk takes on so few new games each year – a mere thirty or forty altogether.

Another delusion that assails so many inventors is that their game has got to be in an advanced state of development before Games Talk will look at it. The very reverse is true; it is only the idea that counts.

The structure and rules for a game can always be devised around a good concept. In fact, it is the potential for this participation in a game's development that Games Talk finds most attractive. It is rare indeed for a game to come to them in a form that is fit for the market. By the time they have spent up to one year developing it, it will probably have changed out of all recognition – the game play, the dynamics, the composition, the componentry, the whole format. But one thing is certain; it will be a much better board game at the end of it and, even more importantly, a marketable commodity containing all the elements that contemporary games manufacturers currently require.

The procedure is straightforward enough. Most games come to Games Talk through the major manufacturers. An inventor sends his game to a toy company that will either re-direct it or advise the originator to do so themselves. Games Talk then looks at it, rejects it, sends the inventor a letter explaining why and charges a service fee of £19.50. End of story. In ninety nine per cent of all cases that is exactly what happens and nothing more. But when it comes to the remaining magical few, a very different scenario unfolds. It is that all-important recognition of originality that sparks it off.

The inventor is invited in for a free consultation to discuss his concept in more detail. Further discussion may take place over a period of several months and the idea explored from every angle. The two parties begin to get to know each other. Finally, once they have both agreed to go ahead, a contract is drawn up and signed between them. It is a symbolic moment.

For a start, the inventor has contracted to pay Games Talk a considerable sum of his own money in exchange for a guarantee that his game will be developed into a working prototype fit for the marketplace. Games Talk will then do everything within its considerable influence to license it to a major manufacturer. From what was a no-hope situation, the inventor now has a one in three chance of seeing his brainchild turned into a commercial product, in all probability making him a lot of money in the process.

The key to the whole formula is joint venture. As Kidney says: "We're only interested in something we are going to invest in ourselves; after all, our success fee is thirty five per cent of the financial rewards." What the inventor pays for is all the material development of the game, right the way through to a full production prototype. This can amount to anything from £1,000 to £6,000 plus VAT, depending on the complexity of the game; but as this sum is estimated in advance, once it has been paid, the inventor's financial involvement is finished. Under no circumstances will he be asked to pay anything more. And as patenting is not considered appropriate for games, he escapes that remorseless treadmill as well.

For their part, Games Talk now begins a process that involves an in-depth study of the game and all its permutations. Its aim is to try to achieve a package that will set it apart from other properties that have preceded it. It is a tall order. As Iain Kidney says: "We try to create a vision for the game, some goal that we can aspire to that will set it apart from all the others. It is the principal objective of the development programme."

Play testing is an integral part of that programme. Games are played in natural environments by non-professionals and their responses monitored very carefully. Is it original? Is it fast? Is it fun? Does it really stand up? What are its weaknesses? All these factors are taken into account, along with other more esoteric details, and once it has been fine-tuned it is submitted again and again for further testing. It is a long process. Finally, a full-scale prototype is made up by professional designers and model-makers and a photograph is taken for the all-important sales portfolio. It always looks splendid and it is a fine moment for the originator.

The sales process is the part that Iain Kidney takes great pride in. Selling a new game to a manufacturer is more difficult than selling the proverbial fridge to an eskimo. But he has known them all for years. He will see most of the major toy companies around the world at least once a year and is in regular contact with them all. He knows exactly the sort of thing that each is looking for and has a fine feel for the latest trends. He targets companies with particular games accordingly. As soon as a manufacturer expresses an interest in a game it is sent the prototype. There is usually only one but it is indistinguishable from the real thing.

Sometimes games hit the mark with more than one manufacturer right away and the prospect of an early sale requires additional models.

But strangely enough some games can do the rounds for years before being taken up. As a result, all games remain in the portfolio for three years before being considered for deletion.

Once a sale is clinched, a licence agreement is drawn up by Games Talk and a royalty rate agreed. This can be anything from eight per cent for a simple game needing little investment to three and a half per cent for a complex one that may require considerable promotion. Sometimes there is an advance on royalties, but more often it is a guaranteed income at the end of the first year. Outright sales are rare.

What in Kidney's view constitutes a good game? "First of all you must have originality at the right price and something that appeals to the broadest possible section of the public. But a game must also have personality. It needs clever features, unusual elements, stunning components and, if you can incorporate a third dimension as well, so much the better. It also needs to be promotable on television."

And what are the rewards for the inventor of an internationally successful board game? "Theoretically, the sky's the limit. The inventors of Trivial Pursuit™ are now multi-millionaires living in the Bahamas, but any top-selling game sold this year could possibly generate six-figure royalties in its first twelve months; after that, who knows?"

British Technology Group

The British Technology Group finds itself in a somewhat invidious position in relation to the private inventor. Of all the organisations that represent inventions, BTG is perhaps best known to the public at large. Consequently inventors tend to contact it at an early stage in the hope of getting some support for their ideas, but in fact it only very rarely considers submissions from individuals. At one time it used to be more open to the approaches of independent inventors, but it now sources nearly all its ideas from academic institutions, research establishments and companies worldwide.

BTG, which floated on the London stock exchange in July 1995, following privatisation in 1992,was set up in 1948 to license out the

148

technology that emerged from research departments of universities, polytechnics and government research establishments throughout the country. The quality and diversity of this research in terms of its commercial potential was enormous; however a problem was that the expertise tended to escape into the public domain, leaving the field clear for foreign competitors.

What happens now is what BTG describes as 'global technology transfer'. Actually it is somewhat more sophisticated than that. In order to cover all its interests, BTG has three separate operating divisions, supported by one of the most sophisticated patent and licensing departments in the world. These divisions cover a wide variety of disciplines. Broadly they are divided into biosciences, engineering and electronics and telecommunication, with BTG currently holding about 9,000 patents in 1,400 technologies.

Once this wealth of intellectual property has been properly secured, BTG vigorously markets the contents of its portfolio to companies around the world and actively seeks licensing opportunities that will bring in revenues to be shared with the originators of the technology. All in all, it makes BTG the largest patenting and licensing organisation worldwide.

But BTG is not unsympathetic towards the independent inventor, sometimes taking on ideas from individuals – although they tend to source them directly. However, in the main, BTG doesn't have the facilities to assess the sort of ideas that private inventors tend to come up with and they are normally referred to the **Institute of Patentees and Inventors** for further advice.

The Design Council

Although the Design Council no longer offers direct design advice or support services to companies and individuals, the organisation still promotes innovation at regional level through the Design Link scheme. This relies on approved local designers providing back-up to the individual Design Consultant appointed by the Business Link. Although the Design Council does not make individual grants, it is responsible for awarding DTI funds under the Special Design Project Funding initiative, which in 1996 handed out a quarter of a million pounds to nine successful projects. (This money is awarded to projects which 'advance the rôle of design in society', and does not apply to individual inventions.)

In addition, the Council runs a programme of collaborative awards, working as consultants to partners in industry, government, education and the design field, to promote standards of excellence and benchmarking in the industry.

The Design Council is still an immensely valuable resource for inventors in terms of historic reference material, publications, contacts and information services. Certainly, without this early example of a 'Quango' in action, Britain would not enjoy the pre-eminent place in world design it holds today.

6

Venture Capitalists
and Business Angels

Venture capital is seldom available from institutional investors,
except for a handful listed elsewhere. Information is available from
the British Venture Capital Association (BVCA), which publishes a
useful *Guide to Venture Capital*. The Association's Directory lists
more than one hundred full members, who between them invest several billion pounds annually, mostly in the United Kingdom. In
1979, when the Association was founded, its members invested a
mere £20 million; it is a huge and growing financial sector which is
particularly well developed in the UK. However, for all its
resources, virtually none of this money – only 7% – is ever targeted
at the independent inventor.

   This is not a criticism; because of the obvious risk involved, only
a very small proportion of venture capital companies have any interest whatever in start-ups – apart perhaps from some technology-
based businesses run by individuals with a good track-record in
industry – and of these, very few offer the sort of seed capital that
would interest an inventor. As BVCA Head of Communications,
Charlotte Morrison, puts it: "Most inventors' weakness is to assume
that because they have a brilliant idea, someone must want to finance
it – without their being prepared, i.e. without a good management
team to turn the product into a commercial reality, without a grasp of

the market and the competition. For inventors who get off the starting blocks and are prepared, there is a variety of capital available to them. The tax incentives available to qualifying companies are attractive. Inventors and their team might do well to see if their business qualifies for this kind of investment before finding a business angel."

The argument is understandable. Even though the investment may be small, the risks are too high and the potential rewards too meagre for the due diligence and the effort needed to monitor it. No matter how promising a project may appear, it is likely to prove a lacklustre investment, at least for the first few years.

Business Angels

Apart from the celestial kind, an 'angel' is usually someone who is prepared to make a personal investment in a theatrical production. Presumably the expression came from the impresario's rapturous reply when told of an individual's intention to do so: "Darling, you're an *angel*!" A business angel does much the same thing, except he or she is interested in a business venture and not a West End show. But if celestial angels are uncommon, business angels are, in the present economic climate, a rare breed indeed. However, there are people out there who walked away with fortunes made in the booming 1980s and they are still looking for somewhere interesting to put their money. All you have to do is find them....

You can advertise for a business angel. Such advertisements appear regularly in the classified pages of the *Financial Times*. Somebody has an idea and is looking for private money to back it. Such people are ready to give away a share of their equity in exchange for an investment. They are probably even prepared to take the backer on board with them and make him a director of the new company.

Investors in such enterprises want to keep a clear eye on their investment and usually insist on becoming closely involved with the company. However, this is often all to the good; business angels have not got money to spare for nothing. They have usually made it through their own industry or investment and are shrewd businessmen. Their experience, as well as their money, can make all the difference to a start-up business venture.

There are at least two organisations that act as agents for entrepreneurs looking for business angels. Each produces its own monthly bulletin outlining the financial requirements of their clients and sends it out to a mailing list of several hundred subscribers who over the years have shown some interest in such investments. On average, each bulletin contains about a dozen proposals, of which between ten and twenty per cent are taken up. The success rate may not seem very high, but the service that each offers to its contributors in helping them to draw up a business plan, for one thing, is invaluable in itself.

The applicant is encouraged to state his requirements in a clear and concise manner and to outline his proposals precisely. It is perhaps the first time he has really been called upon to focus on what he is about. It can concentrate the mind wonderfully and, even if he fails to find a business partner, he may come to see his own position much more clearly. In each case the cost is extremely reasonable.

For an individual inventor starting up with a new idea, a business angel may be premature, but if his product is up-and-running and has already made a niche for itself in the marketplace, he may well find just what he wants through *Venture Capital Report* or **LINC**. In some respects, it is the purest route to venture capital and, if he finds an empathy with his 'angel', it could well turn out to be a marriage made in heaven.

Venture Capital Report

Had Lucius Cary been a more conventional entrepreneur, he might by now be resting on his laurels, not to mention a sizeable sum of money, as the hamburger tycoon of the 'eighties. In 1972, he saw the commercial possibilities of high quality American hamburgers sold in a pop-style diner, quick service restaurant. It is a formula others have since found hugely profitable. By 1977 he had three restaurants and a staff of fifty. His investors were convinced they had backed a winner, but they had not reckoned with their young entrepreneur and his peculiar proclivities. Sitting in his office atop his money machine downstairs, he dreamed up a scheme to help others raise capital for similar start-ups, or indeed any other business activity they might have in mind. Thus was founded **Venture Capital Report.**

Eventually Cary bought out his backers and sold the restaurant business to concentrate all his effort on *VCR*. At first it was tough going. How do you get advertisers to advertise in a magazine that does not exist or subscribers to subscribe to a periodical with no editorial? However, through a series of judicious advertisements in the *Financial Times*, he eventually attracted six contributors and compiled detailed reports on their requirements. These made up the first *VCR* in 1978; it sold a mere fifteen copies. His breakthrough came when an early contributor attracted the money he required and the *FT* wrote an article about it. At last he was on his way.

Over the years *VCR* has grown into an established monthly bulletin containing around ten new business proposals in each issue and sent out to over eight hundred regular subscribers. At first it was hoped that the magazine could survive on subscriptions alone, but advertisers now pay £350 for an entry, plus a further 'success fee' of £1,000, plus two and a half percent of the capital raised. For performing what for many an aspiring entrepreneur must seem little short of magic, this by most standards is a modest price to pay.

As a result of its reputation, *VCR* now receives perhaps two and a half thousand approaches each year from inventors seeking to raise capital for their business ventures. After meeting about two hundred of them and discussing their requirements at length, around half are eventually published in *VCR*, giving a detailed account of their proposals. On average, each article receives around three or four enquiries. The success rate is roughly ten per cent or around one start-up per month being backed, while another ten per cent ultimately find their funding elsewhere.

Each application for inclusion in the bulletin is vetted carefully for its viability. Once accepted for consideration, the entrepreneur is invited to *VCR*'s offices in Oxford and an article is written for the report based on the detailed information the individual gives about himself and his requirements. The object is to provide as much factual information as an investor might reasonably need to make a judgement. If the business is already trading, then a current balance sheet is provided, together with cash flow projections. Each article runs to around four or five pages, together with pictures, and is approved by the entrepreneur. It ends with the name and address of the entrepreneur, enabling investors to get in touch directly.

Cary sold *VCR* in 1996, as he says it never made any money, but has stayed on as Chairman of the company. He has a clear vision of his target audience: "We are out to attract business angels who have a certain amount of money to invest in a venture. Sometimes these people are very rich, with more than £10 million to invest – others may have half a million or so – but most have limited resources and are looking to give themselves a new role and interest in life and to be very much part of the operation into which they are putting their money. Often they have considerable business experience to bring to bear and their investment is only part of their contribution."

An investor who is interested makes direct contact with the entrepreneur. Although *VCR* remains available for further guidance to either side, it takes no formal part in drawing up an agreement between them. Many of the projects that attract support from business angels in this way go on to achieve considerable commercial success, but one of Cary's abiding disappointments is how few of his proposals find a backer: "I am often surprised by the ideas that do get taken up, but I am frequently even more surprised by those that don't." Indeed. according to a Bank of England report, published in October 1996, UK investors put only a third as much money into new technology start-ups as their American counterparts; while the *Financial Times* quoted a BVCA report estimating that only seven per cent of UK investment capital goes to start-ups. Nevertheless, the situation is slowly improving, and Cary can take a lot of the credit for popularising 'seedcorn capitalism' in the UK.

Seed Capital Ltd.

Cary's long-running fund, Seed Capital grew out of his frustration at seeing good ideas starved of cash. He believed strongly that with the right financial and managerial support some of these little enterprises could be turned into really profitable companies. The problem was choosing which ones. The only way to find out was to invest in a basket of ideas himself with at least sufficient funds to get them going... As luck would have it, he found himself in the early 'eighties sharing a London office with a progressive venture capital company. He eventually persuaded the directors to let him manage a fund of £200,000 to put his ideas into practice.

Ten years later he is on to his sixth fund and he has made a total of forty three investments, the first forty being all of less than £50,000, although more recent ventures have involved larger amounts, typically of up to a quarter of a million pounds, reflecting an increaing bias towards technology. Says Cary: "What I am looking for is a really innovative product at a very early stage of development, perhaps only a concept that is looking promising. If I have faith in the individuals involved, I will back them to the point where they can develop a prototype and set themselves up in limited production with their idea. What we want is some feedback from the marketplace to see whether we are on the right track.

"I set a ceiling on each project in order to limit the risk. It is all-too easy to get sucked into an ever-increasing investment. But through *Venture Capital Report* and other contacts I have in the industry, I am usually able to find second stage funding from another source if necessary.

"The other important thing is, I have to see some light at the end of the tunnel before I go into it. I am not interested in black holes. The exit point is of paramount importance, although it is always some years down the track. Of course, some companies don't last very long and I lose my money, but so far we have managed to make a profit and if one in ten turns out to be a real winner I shall be more than happy. In all cases I expect the entrepreneur to buy out my equity in the company after ten years."

Oxford Technology Venture Capital Trust

Lucius Cary's latest venture is Oxford Technology VCT, set up in March 1997 with a fund of about £3 million to invest in early-stage and start-up technology companies in and around Oxford. Founded in conjunction with Larpent Newton, part of Friends Provident, the Trust aims to provide equity capital of between £100,000 and £500,000 – although, says Cary, he will consider smaller amounts.

LINC/Local Investment Networking Company

One of the perennial problems faced by entrepreneurs is the equity gap between the original start-up cost of a small business and the capital required for subsequent expansion. The sum ranges roughly between £10,000 and £250,000, depending on the size and type of business. Too small usually to interest the venture capital institutions, these sums are well within what individual business angels are willing and able to invest in an attractive business venture, in exchange for some personal stake and involvement in the company. The problem, however, is matching their money with the right business opportunity.

LINC – the Local Investment Networking Company –was founded by the London Enterprise Agency (LEntA) in the 1980s and later became a separate limited company offering a national service, matching companies seeking equity finance to private investors with good, commercially-sound ideas. 'Business angels'are usually energetic and entrepreneurial people who have made money in the past through their own endeavours. They are generally well qualified to take the helm of a promising new company. However, in much the same way that small businesses find new funding hard to come by, so business angels need an accredited source of investment opportunities to resource. LINC's principal method of marketing these opportunities to interested investors is through *LINC Bulletin*, published every month. Each issue contains around thirty new business opportunities. (Since 1995, LINC and *Venture Capital Report* have cooperated in carrying summaries of projects appearing in one anothers'publications.)

Companies wishing to be included in the *Bulletin* can contact LINC through their nationwide network of member agents, based at local Business Link centres. Their expert business advisers will assess the applicant's suitability for the LINC scheme. LINC also operates a contacts database, and maximises its networking opportunities through regular investor meetings and Investor Club seminars.

Susan Krantz is the General Manager, administering LINC from its head office in London She is responsible for editing the *Bulletin* and sending it out to more-than three hundred current subscribers. As she explains: "Our subscribers are actively looking for an investment and it is normal for a good opportunity to be taken up quite quickly. In fact, we are encouraged by our success rate, which runs at around ten to fifteen per cent. Much of this is due to the activities of our local member agents. In fact, over £6 million has been invested in businesses since LINC started.

"There is a lot of hard work involved in getting an investor to commit to a new idea. It is a serious long-term investment."

Once an introduction has been effected between the two parties, LINC stands back and allows negotiations to take their course, based on the advice from the respective professional advisers, accountants and solicitors. Investors are required to carry out their own due diligence on the company, and LINC plays no part in drawing up the agreement. Investors seldom want a controlling interest in a company – the norm is around a quarter to a third of the equity in return for their investment, depending on the volume of business and the negotiating skills of the parties concerned. If they decide to participate actively in the company, they can of course negotiate a director's salary.

"There is no blueprint for our average investor", concludes Krantz. "The only thing that they have in common is money. It is our job to match them up with those who need it."

Korda & Co.

Alongside the major city institutions, the venture capital field has a flourishing 'fringe' of small companies and individuals with access to private investment channels and small 'pots' of money – the problem being, that these contacts are hard to find; their finances fluctuate, their aims are continuously changing and companies come and go.

If your invention can fairly be described as a leading-edge technological breakthrough with substantial commercial potential, then Alex Korda might be your man. Korda makes only one or two new investments each year and consequently is very selective. But if he has faith in both you and your technology you might well find he has the right contacts to help you exploit it. Says Korda: "Korda and Co. is now just a virtual company. It was originally set up in 1989 to manage a number of specific projects, and these have been largely successful; but the fund is now being wound down and will cease to exist from 1999. Consequently I am not taking on any new projects through the company at the moment."

However, Alex Korda is still very much in the venture capital business on his own account, and is hoping to launch a new $100 million Technology fund in the very near future. "What we look for is a proposal from a leading researcher in his field suggesting there might be a new or better way of achieving a result for which there is a clear commercial need and from which we can build a business to satisfy that need. I am always open to ideas and concepts that, if properly exploited, have the potential to convert into many millions of pounds within a reasonable period of time." But, Korda warns, "Of course, the individuals concerned have got to be of an outstanding calibre from a scientific point of view and ideally should have had some commercial experience as well."

StratCap

Based in the cathedral town of Winchester, Hampshire, StratCap (short for Strategic Capital), is primarily engaged in strategy and organisational development. Set up by Richard Hardy nine years ago, its purpose is to provide management consulting skills to young companies with high growth potential concerned with creating and commercialising new products. However, with the right project in view,

StratCap will aim to find sources of seed capital from within the venture capital industry to enable this process to take place. Says Hardy: "We provide a hands-on service and are closely involved with the company through all its stages of development. Once we have the money in place, we help to build the organisation from within in partnership with the entrepreneur. We are only interested in setting up companies with a very high growth rate potential."

Since 1995, StratCap has gone on the back burner as Hardy has been involved more with the consultancy side, and there is at present only a single long-term project still under management. However, Richard Hardy says that StratCap is still very much in business in the long run and he anticipates an increased level of activity in 1998/9.

For the innovator/entrepreneur, one of the most attractive elements of the StratCap approach is the very low equity stake it requires in exchange for its services. Initial consultation with the client is free, which enables Hardy to pick up the ideas he wants to pursue. But even then he operates on a contingency, 'no success, no fee' basis, until the right funding has been put in place, whereupon he takes a modest success fee from his client. To ensure a high level of motivation, he insists that the entrepreneur retains the majority shareholding in the new company, and once the division of equity between the investor and the company has been agreed, he only requires around ten per cent of the inventor's stake for the services he provides.

Although StratCap is not a member of the BVCA, it may well be a valuable port of call for the innovator when it is considered how hard it is to obtain venture capital elsewhere. If Hardy really believes in you and your idea, he will do all he can to raise the funds required to carry your idea forward into commercial production, and then stay with it every step of the way. His aim is to make sure you are running your company effectively, because his vested interest is wholly tied up with your ultimate success. To that end, StratCap will also consider putting in qualified management to grow the business

But Hardy offers a final word of warning: "I don't expect people to come to me with some half-baked idea on the back of an envelope. I do expect them to have thought through their proposals very carefully, or we are just wasting one another's time."

Appendix

Useful Addresses and Contact Numbers

NOTE

While the Publishers have taken reasonable care to ensure that the information given in this section is up-to-date and accurate at the time of going to press, addresses and telephone numbers (and the aims, scope, methods, costs, names of individuals, grants, and other details given about companies and organisations mentioned in this book) are subject to a continuous process of change. Readers are strongly advised to make enquiries and seek independent advice before entering into contractual arrangements of any kind.

Barnsley Business & Innovation Centre
Innovation Way, Barnsley, S.Yorks S75 1JS
Tel: 01226 249590 Fax: 01226 249625

BEST (Building Expertise in Science & Technology)
Cartermill International Ltd, Technology Centre, St Andrews,
Fife KY16 9EA
Tel: 01334 477660 Fax: 01334 477180

British Technology Group Ltd
101 Newington Causeway, London SE1 6BU
Tel: 0171 403 6666 Fax: 0171-403 7586

British Venture Capital Association
Essex House, 12-13 Essex Street, London WC2R 3AA
Tel: 0171-240 3846 Fax: 071-240 3849

Business Link (Technology and Innovation Service)
See your local telephone directory. Information also from the DTI.

Chartered Institute of Patent Agents
Staple Inn Buildings, High Holborn, London WC1V 7PZ
Tel: 0171-405 9450 Fax: 0171-430 0471

Chartered Society of Designers
32-38 Saffron Hill, London EC1N 8FH
Tel: 0171-831 9777 Fax: 0171-831 6277

Confederation of British Industry (CBI)
Centre Point, 103 New Oxford Street, London WC1A 1DU
Tel: 0171 379 7400 Fax: 0171-240 1578

Department of Trade & Industry
151 Buckingham Palace Road, London SW1W 9SS
Tel: 0171 215 5000 Fax: 0171-215 0105

The Design Council
Haymarket House, 1 Oxendon Street, London W1Y 4EE
Tel: 0171-208 2121 Fax: 0171-839 6033

European Business & Innovation Centres Network
Headquartered in Brussels, there are 11 EBI Centres in the UK:
Staffordshire (01785 226598), S. Yorkshire (01226 249590), Greater
Manchester (0161-337 8648), Cardiff (01222 372311), Birmingham
(0121-359 0981), Cambridge (01223 420252), Londonderry (01504
264242), Wrexham (01978 290694), Blackburn (01254 692692),
Enfield (0181-805 8100) and Sunderland (01915 160222).

Games Talk
Little Coster, Blunsdon Hill, Swindon, Wilts SN2 4BZ
Tel: 01793 705291 Fax: 01793 705292

Gloucestershire Business Link
Chalgrove House, Shurdington, Glos.
Tel: 01452 509560 (Direct Line) Fax: 01452 509500

Grantfinder
Contact Business Links
(e.g. Gloucestershire Business Link - see above)

Industrial Design Consultancy Ltd
Portland Business Centre, Manor House Lane, Datchet,
Slough SL3 9EG
Tel: 01753 547610 Fax: 01753 549224

Industrial Research and Development Unit – Northern Ireland
Netherleigh, Massey Avenue, Belfast BT8
Tel: 01232 529385 Fax: 01232 529548

Innovations Group Ltd
211 Lower Richmond Road, Richmond, Surrey TW9 4LN
Tel: 0181-727 3000 Fax: 0181-727 3222

Institute of Directors
116 Pall Mall, London SW1Y 5ED
Tel: 0171 839 1233 Fax: 0171-930 1949

Institute of Patentees and Inventors
Suite 505a, Triumph House, 189 Regent Street, London W1R 7WF
Tel: 0171 242 7812 Fax: 0171 434 1727

Inventorlink Ltd
5 Clipstone Street, London W1P 7EB
Tel: 0171-323 4323 Fax: 0171-323 0286

Korda and Co. Ltd (Alex Korda)
Outer Temple, 222 The Strand, London WC2R 1DE
Tel: 0171-583 3377

LEDU (Local Enterprise Development Unit) – Northern Ireland
Ledger House, Upper Galwally, Belfast BT8 4TB
Tel: 01232 491031 Fax: 01232 691432

Lenton Manufacturing & Technology Unit
Lenton Business Centre, Lenton Boulevard, Nottingham NG7 2BY
Tel: 0115-955 2107 Fax: 0115-955 2108

LINC – Local Investment Networking Co.
4 Snow Hill, London EC1A 2BS
Tel: 0171-332 0877 Fax: 0171-329 0226

London Enterprise Agency
LentA Ltd, 4 Snow Hill, London EC1A 2BS
Tel: 0171-236 3000 Fax: 0171-329 0226

Lyons Ames
63 Farringdon Road, London EC1M 3JB
Tel: 0171-404 0407 Fax: 0171-405 0365

NatWest UK – Innovation and Growth Unit
Level 10, Drapers Gardens, 12 Throgmorton Avenue,
London EC2N 2DL.
Tel: 0171-454 2432 Fax: 0171 454 2610

North East Innovation Centre Company Ltd
Neilson Road, Gateshead, Tyne & Wear NE10 0EW
Tel: 0191-478 3639 Fax: 0191 478 3639

Oxford Health Care Ltd
259 Woodstock Road, Oxford OX2 7AE
Tel: 01865 558604

Pankhurst Design and Developments
286 Munster Road, London SW6 6BQ
Tel: 0171-381 6155 Fax: 0171 381 9475

Patent Office
Cardiff Road, Newport, Gwent NP9 1RH
Tel: 01633 813535

Patent Library
c/o The British Science Reference Library
25 Southampton Buildings, Chancery Lane, London WC2A 1AD

Pax Technology Transfer Ltd
112 Boundary Road, London NW8 0RH
Tel: 0171-328 9649 Fax: 0171-328 9519

Prince of Wales Award for Innovation
44, Baker Street, London W1A 1DH
Tel: 0171-224 1600 Fax: 0171-486 1700

Product First Ltd
10 Barley Mow Passage, Chiswick, London W4 4PH
Tel: 0181-994 6477 Fax: 0181 742 1886

Product International Ltd
Field House, Mount Road, Stone, Staffs ST15 8LJ
Tel: 01785 818155 Fax: 01785 817244

Sams Design
103 Friern Barnet Rd, London N11 3EU
Tel: 0181 361 8845 Fax: 0181 361 4305

SCEPTRE (Sheffield Innovation Centre)
Hallam University, Pond Street, Sheffield S1 1WB
Tel: 0114-272 0911 Fax: 0114-253 3352

Scottish Enterprise
120 Bothwell Street, Glasgow G2 7JP
Tel: 0141-248 2700 Fax:0141 221 3217

Scottish Innovation
Templeton Business Centre, 62 Templeton Street, Glasgow G40 1DA
Tel: 0141-554 5995 Fax: 0141-556 6320

Seven Towns Ltd
7 Lambton Place, London W11 2SH
Tel: 0171-727 5666 Fax: 0171-221 0363

SMART awards
Management & Technology Services Division
Fourth Floor, DTI, 151 Buckingham Palace Road,
London SW1W 9SS
Tel: 0171-215 5000 Fax: 0171: 215 0105

StratCap
St Thomas' House, St Thomas' Street, Winchester, Hants
Tel: 01962 868779 Fax: 01962 840030

The Technology Exchange
Wrest Park, Silsoe, Bedford MK45 4HS
Tel: 01525 860333 Fax: 01525 860664

Venture Capital Report/ Seed Capital Ltd
The Magdalene Centre, Oxford Science Park, 0X4 4GA
Tel: 01865 784411 Fax: 01865 784412

Wharmby Associates
1 Bonny Street, London NW1 9PE
Tel: 0171-482 4866 Fax: 0171-267 7925

Index